Rainy Days in Texas Funbook

Wallace O. Chariton
Introduction by Jennifer L. Chariton

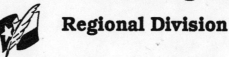

Wordware Publishing, Inc.
Regional Division

Library of Congress Cataloging-In-Publication Data

Charlton, Wallace O.
Rainy days in Texas funbook.

Summary: Puzzles, games, and trivia questions introduce the history, symbols, and people of Texas.
1. Texas—Miscellanea—Juvenile literature. 2. Games Juvenile literature. 3. Puzzles—Juvenile literature.
[1. Texas—Miscellanea. 2. Games. 3. Puzzles]
I. Title.
F386.6.C45 1989 976.4 89-70622
ISBN 1-55622-130-4

1506 Capital Avenue
Plano, Texas 75074

Printed in the United States of America

ISBN 1-55622-130-4
10 9 8 7 6 5 4 3 2

9010

All inquiries for volume purchases of this book should be addressed to Wordware Publishing, Inc., at the above address. Telephone inquiries may be made by calling:

(214) 423-0090

Introduction

Howdy,

My Dad has written many books on Texas, so you could say he knows quite a bit about this subject! I believe that he wrote this book because he loves the great state of Texas so much. He wanted young people to have a workbook that was both fun and educational because he wants young people to know as much as possible about Texas.

Many activities in this book will teach you something very interesting about the Lone Star State. Like me, you probably won't know all the answers, so don't hesitate to get your parents' help.

Many times, I have wondered what to do or complained that I was bored. Well, those days are over for a while. Now that I have this book, I don't think I'll be bored for a long, long time.

Inside this "funbook" you will find many interesting games to make and play. There are also puzzles to solve, challenges to take, and lots of things to color. You can even learn how to read brands on cows. You can also make some great signs for your room, two of which are already hanging on my door!

I won't tell you my favorite activities from the book. By the time you have finished the projects, games, and activities in this book, you will have found your own favorites. I really think you'll enjoy this book as much as I do. Best of luck and remember, follow all instructions carefully. I hope you have a lot of fun with this book and that you learn some new things about Texas because that will make my Dad very happy.

Sincerely,

Jennifer Chariton

Jennifer L. Chariton

P.S. Don't forget to follow the rules my dad has written for you. Like all parents, he's great at making rules!

please . . .

Read this first!

Congratulations! You now have a genuine Texas Funbook. Inside you will find a wonderland of games, puzzles, color pages, and interesting challenges. But, before you start, here are some general rules you should always follow:

First: Always ask your parents' permission before starting any exercise in this book.

Second: Some of the things you will make can be hung up in your room. Be sure to get your parents' permission before hanging anything.

Third: If you have problems with any project, please ask for help from your parents.

Fourth: If your parents do help you with a project, remember to say thank you. A big hug would also be nice.

Fifth: After working on any project, be sure to clean up your mess and put your supplies in a place where you can find them next time.

Sixth: If your parents have rules for using materials needed for completing any project, be sure to follow those rules.

Seventh: For coloring pages, use only crayons or colored pencils. Markers might run through the paper and ruin your drawing.

Eighth: The most important rule of all is be sure to have lots of fun when working on any project in this book.

Ok, now let the fun start!

Before you begin . . .

Since the chances are good someone gave you this book as a present, it is important that you say thanks, Texas style. So, for your first project, here's a special "thank you," card that you can make. All you have to do is cut out the card, color the "thank you," and then write a special message on the back inside the outline of Texas. Next, fold the card along the dotted line, put it in an envelope, address the envelope to whomever gave you the book, put a stamp on it, and drop it in the mailbox. You can be sure that the person who gave you the book will really appreciate getting this personal thank you note.

thank you

Write your special thank you note inside the outline of the state of Texas. Turn the paper around so you write your message from the top. Be sure to mention the book so the person who gave it to you will know what you are thanking them for.

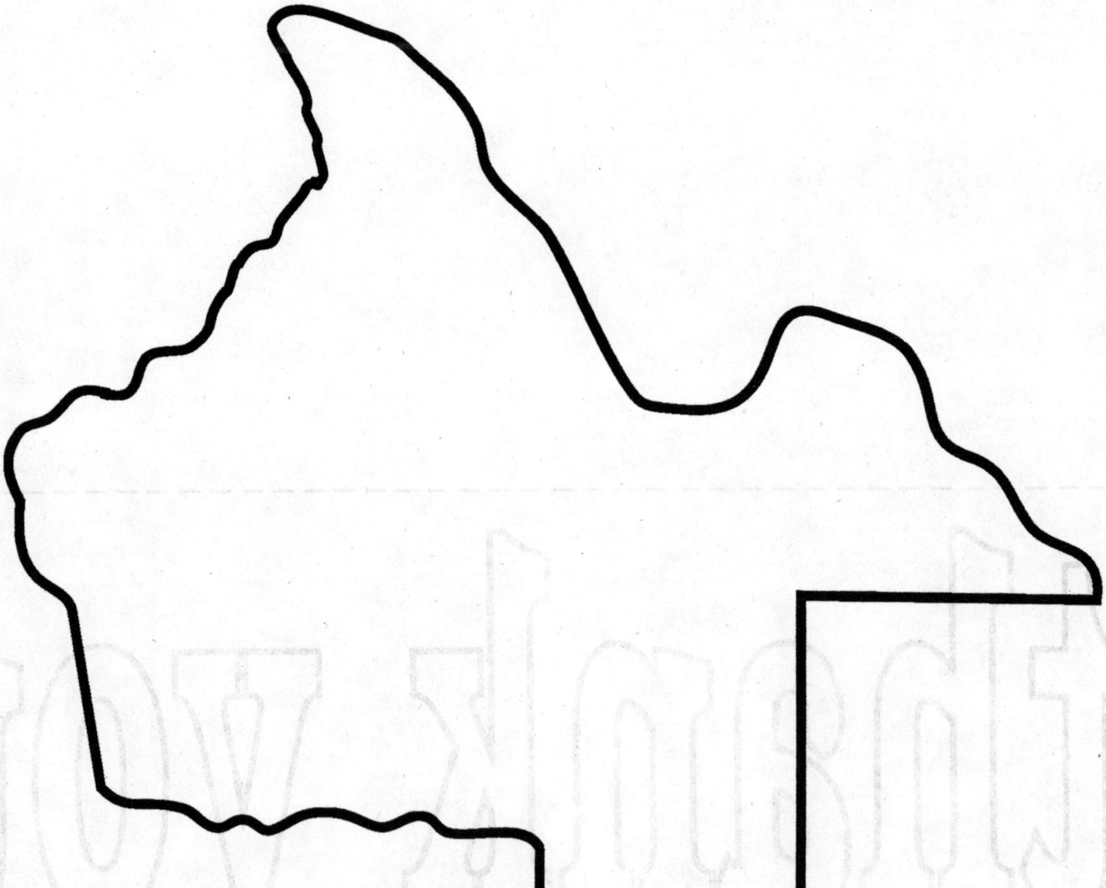

Texas

Colors

Before you color anything, please read this page.

On the pages that follow, you will find some great pictures to test your coloring skill. Please use crayons or colored pencils since markers might run through the pages and ruin your picture. Also, some of the pictures are real challenges because the area to be colored is very small. You will have a much better picture if you keep a sharp point on your crayon or pencil. Work slowly, be careful, and you will have some great pictures that you can be proud of. If you really do your best work, who knows, one of your parents might want to hang a picture somewhere. Good Luck!

As you work through this book you will notice that most of the headlines, like the one above, are in open type. You can color them if you like. You will also find many illustrations that can be colored included in other parts of the book. And finally, in the games you can make, you will want to color certain sections. If you like to use crayons or colored pencils, you will find lots to do in the book.

Texas County Coloring Page

The state of Texas is the second largest state in the United States but Texas has more individual counties than any other state. If you want to find out how many counties Texas has, practice your counting skill and count the counties in the map below. (The answer is in the back of the book.) After counting, you can color the map. If you have the largest set of colors, you can make each county a different color. If you don't have the large set, or if you prefer, color the map so that no counties which touch each other are the same color. Good Luck!

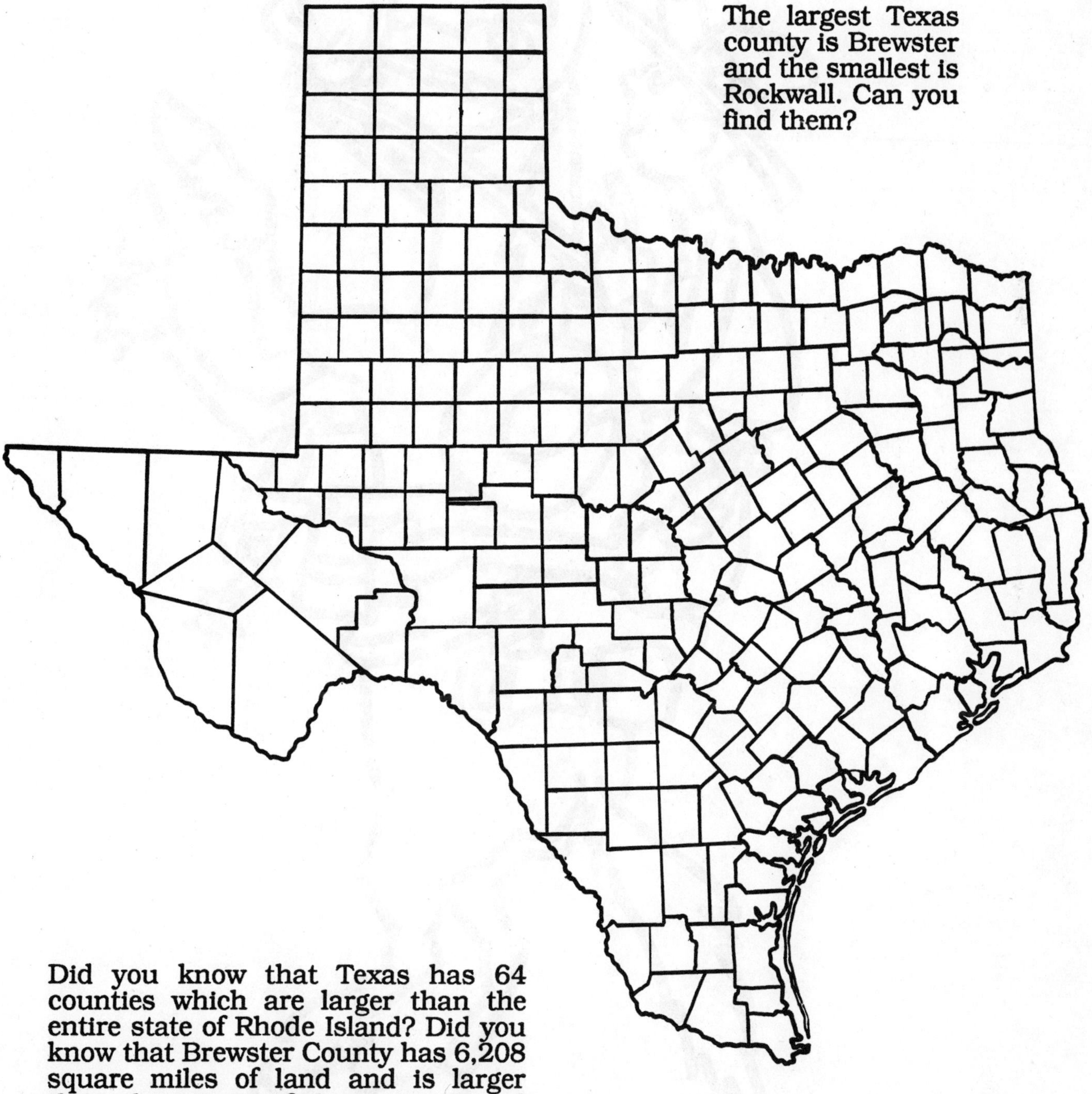

The largest Texas county is Brewster and the smallest is Rockwall. Can you find them?

Did you know that Texas has 64 counties which are larger than the entire state of Rhode Island? Did you know that Brewster County has 6,208 square miles of land and is larger than the states of Connecticut and Rhode Island combined, with plenty of room to spare?

Texas Cowboy Coloring Page

Texas Cowboy Coloring Page

ZZZ

Texas Cowboy Coloring Page

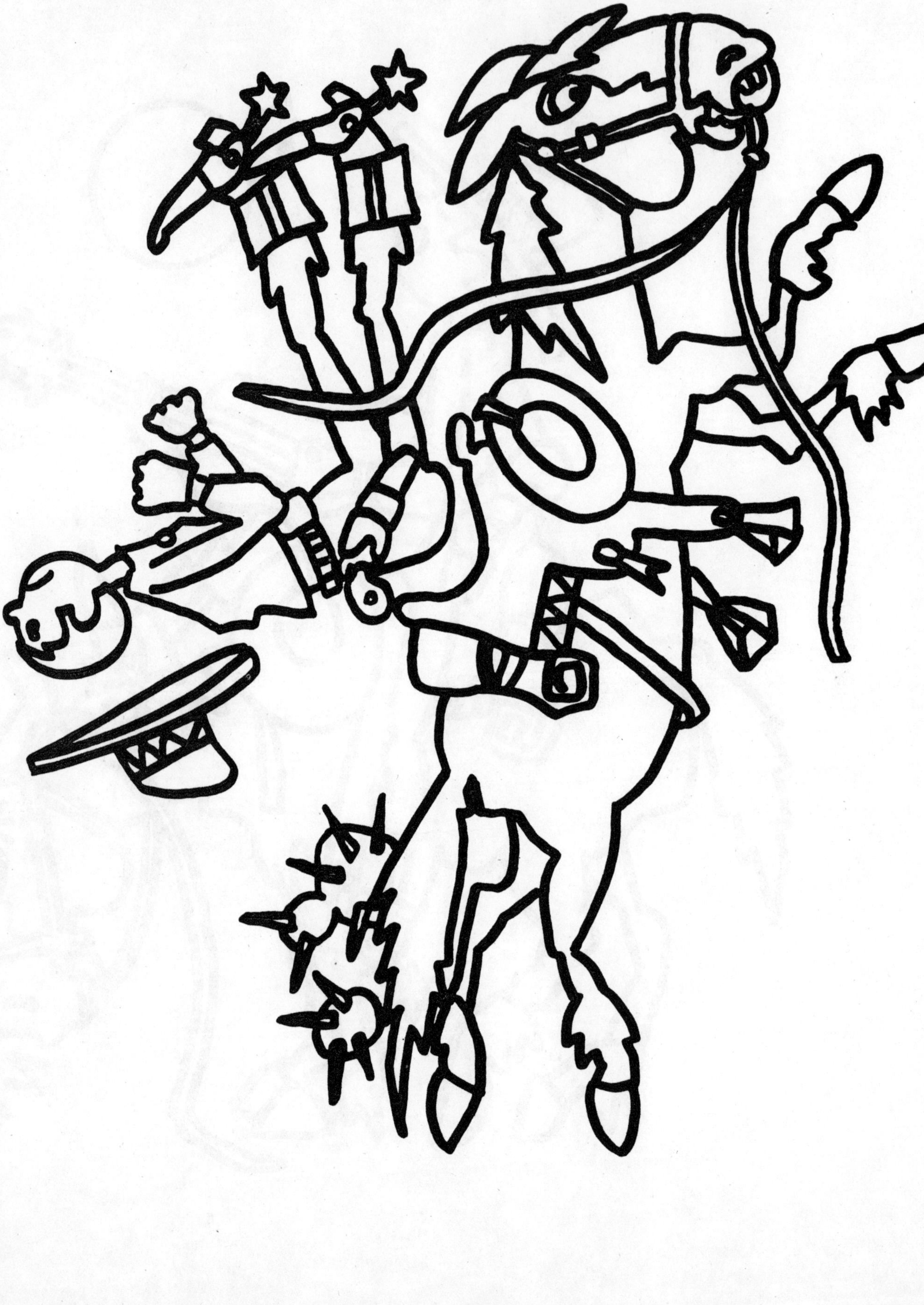

Texas Cowboy Coloring Page

Texas Cowboy Coloring Page

Texas Cowboy Coloring Page

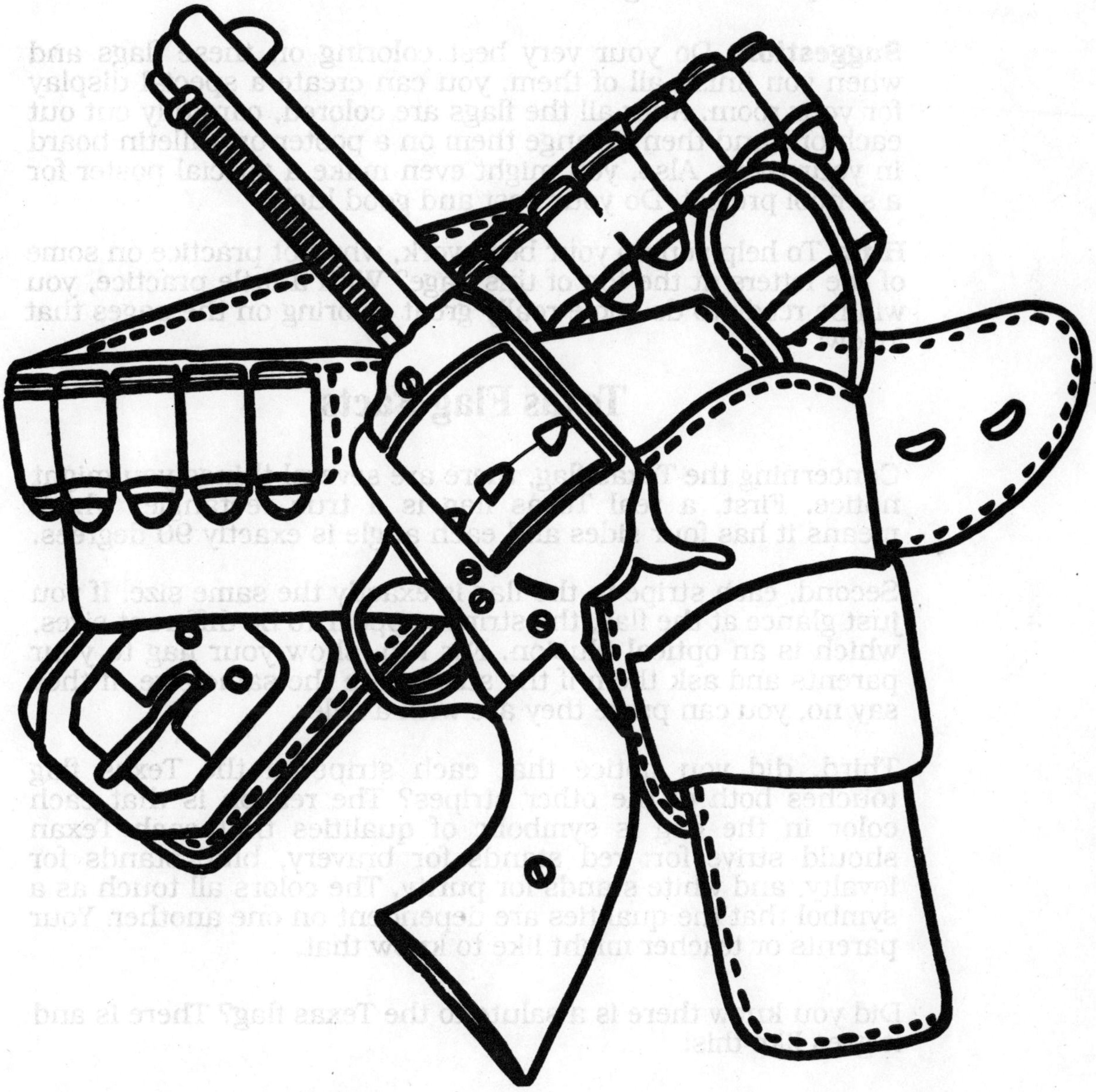

Coloring the flags of Texas

You may have heard that six flags have officially flown over Texas and that is true. However, there have been many others flags used throughout the history of this land called Texas. On the pages that follow, you will find some of the more famous Texas flags, all ready for you to color. Each flag has instructions for you to follow. You can make your flags exactly like the original.

Suggestion: Do your very best coloring on these flags and when you finish all of them, you can create a special display for your room. After all the flags are colored, carefully cut out each one and then arrange them on a poster or bulletin board in your room. Also, you might even make a special poster for a school project. Do your best and good luck.

Hint: To help you do your best work, why not practice on some of the letters at the top of this page? With a little practice, you will be ready to do some really great coloring on the pages that follow!

Texas Flag Facts

Concerning the Texas flag, there are several things you might notice. First, a real Texas flag is a true rectangle, which means it has four sides and each angle is exactly 90 degrees.

Second, each stripe in the flag is exactly the same size. If you just glance at the flag, the stripes appear to be different sizes, which is an optical illusion. For fun, show your flag to your parents and ask them if the stripes are the same size. If they say no, you can prove they are with a ruler.

Third, did you notice that each stripe in the Texas flag touches both of the other stripes? The reason is that each color in the flag is symbolic of qualities that each Texan should strive for: red stands for bravery, blue stands for loyalty, and white stands for purity. The colors all touch as a symbol that the qualities are dependent on one another. Your parents or teacher might like to know that.

Did you know there is a salute to the Texas flag? There is and it goes like this:

"Honor to the Texas Flag!
We pledge our loyalty to
Texas, one and indivisible."

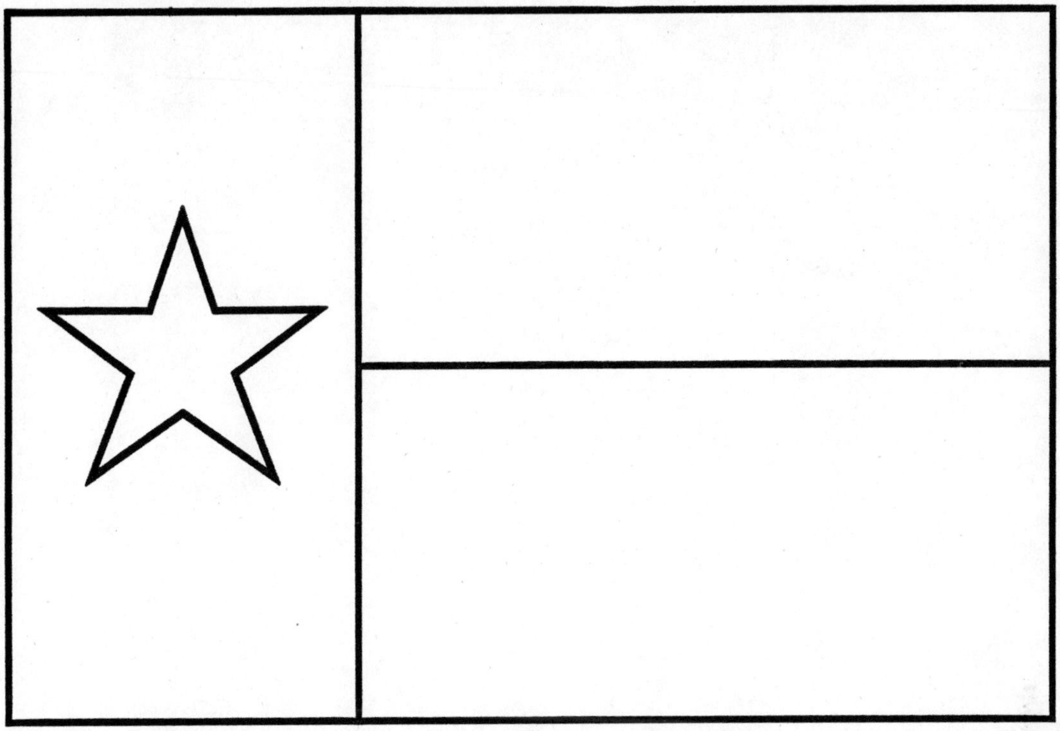

This is the famous "Lone Star" flag of Texas. To color it, the star is white and the background behind the star is blue. The top stripe is white and the bottom stripe is red.

Some Rules for using the Texas Flag

When the flag is flown horizontally, the red stripe of the Texas flag should always be on the bottom.

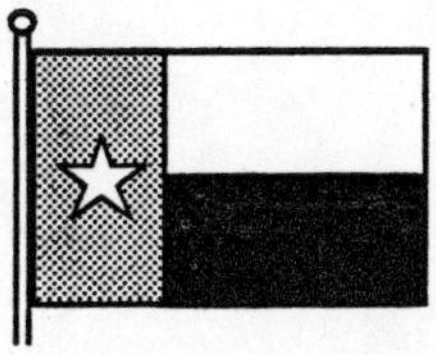

When the flag is shown vertically, as it might be if hung on a wall in your school, the red stripe should be to the left.

When flown with the American flag, the Texas flag should be on the left pole. However, the poles should be of equal length and both flags should be about the same size.When flown from the same pole, the Texas flag should be below the American flag.

The Texas flag should not be flown during bad weather such as rain, hail, sleet, or snow.

The Texas flag should not be flown at night unless lighted.

Every school in Texas should fly the Texas flag on all regular school days.

The Texas Flag should never be allowed to touch the ground and should always be treated with respect, dignity and care.

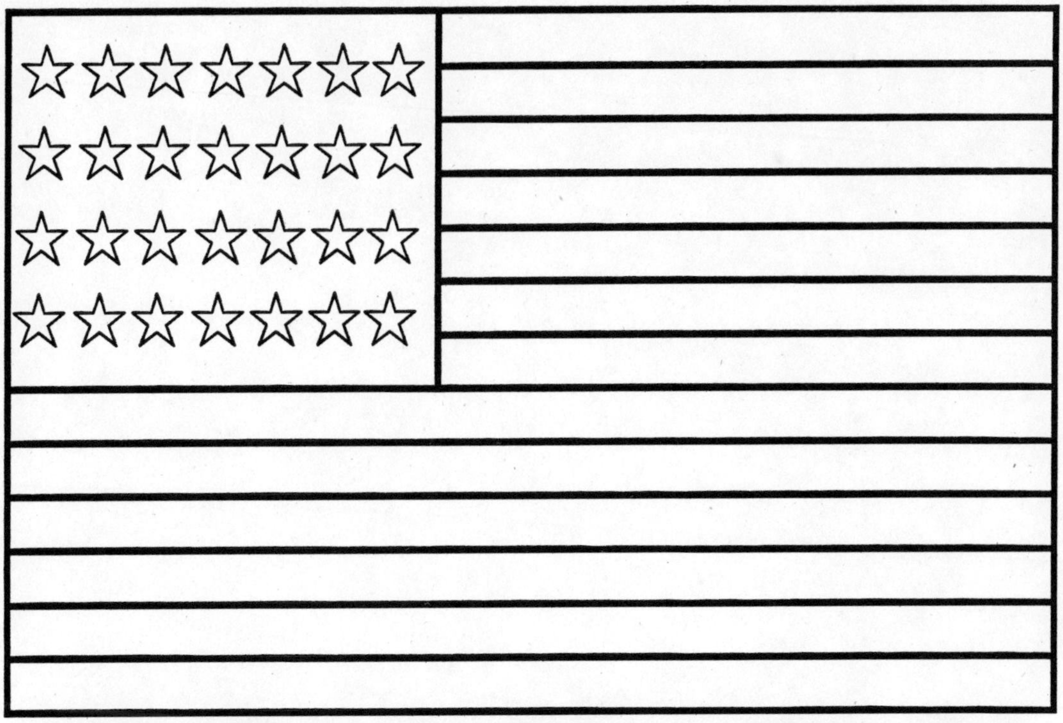

In 1846, the Republic of Texas joined the United States. This is the first U.S. flag to fly over Texas and if you count the number of stars, you will know how many states there were when Texas joined the Union. To color this flag, the background behind the stars is blue and the stars are white. The stripes are red and white, beginning with red at the top.

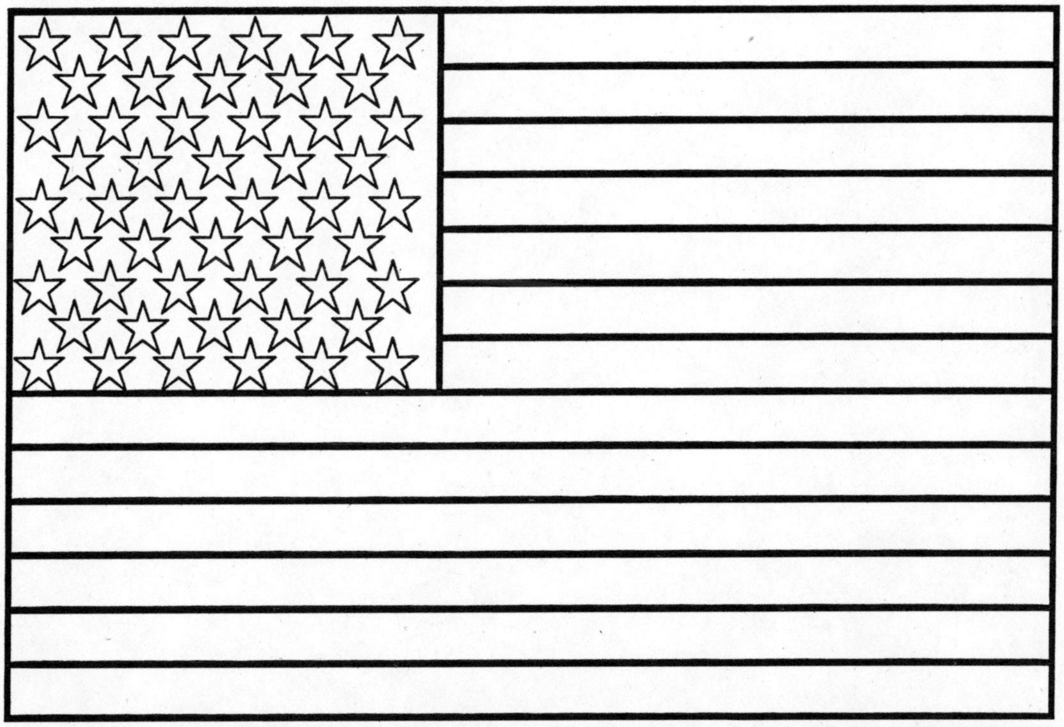

Today, this U.S. flag flies over Texas. If you count the number of stars, you will know how many states there are in the United States. Also, if you count the number of stripes, you will know how many original colonies there were when the United States was first formed. Color this flag like the one above.

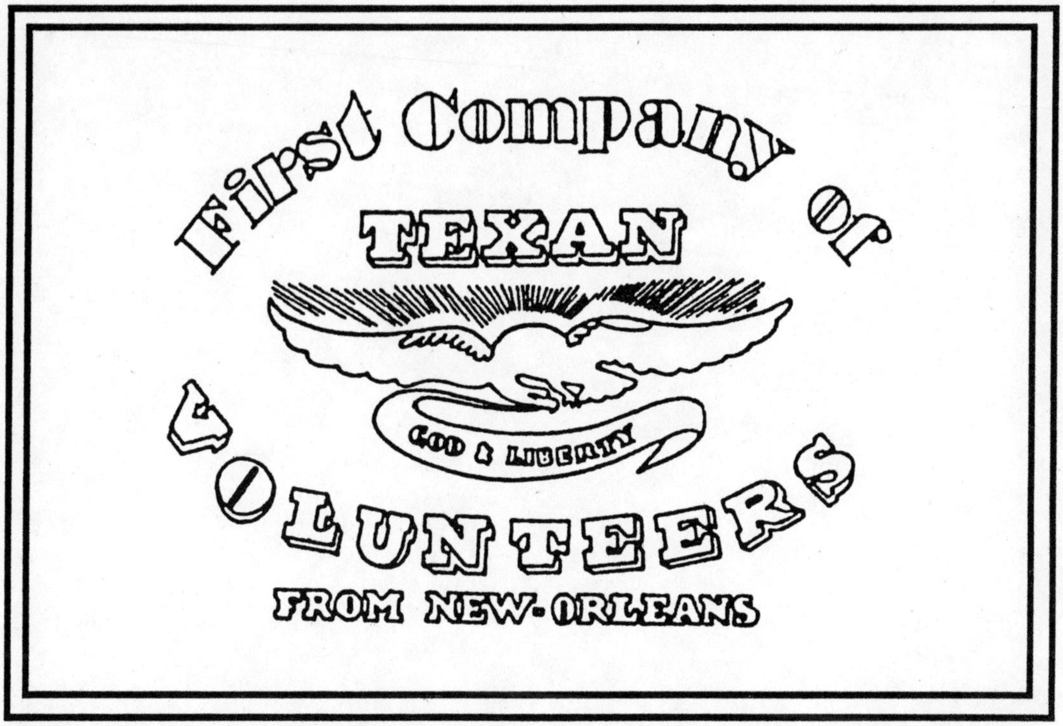
First Company of
TEXAN
GOD & LIBERTY
VOLUNTEERS
FROM NEW-ORLEANS

This flag was captured at the Alamo and sent to Mexico where it remains to this day. To color the flag, make the border gold and the background blue. The words Texan and Volunteers should be black with a white border. All other letters and the eagle are solid black. The banner in the eagle's mouth is white with black letters.

LIBERTY
OR DEATH

This is the flag that was carried at the battle of San Jacinto when Texas won independence. To color the flag, start with the border, which is gold. The background is tan, the lady is flesh and her hair is gold. The lady's gown is white and her cape is red. The sword is silver, the staff is brown, the banner is white and the cloud is gray.

This is the Mexican flag which flew over Texas when Mexico won independence from Spain in 1821. The left stripe is green, the center stripe is white, and the right stripe is red. The eagle and the snake it is holding are brown and the branches are green.

1824

When Santa Anna was elected president of Mexico, he threw out the Mexican constitution of 1824 and became a dictator. This flag was used by Texans and Mexicans who wanted the constitution restored. Color the stripes the same as above except with black numbers.

This is a Spanish flag that was used when Texas was considered a part of Spain. To color this flag, make both of the castles gold and the background behind them red. Color both of the lions red, with gold crowns, and leave the background behind them white.

This is an early French flag that was used when Texas was considered to be a part of France. To color this flag, make the designs gold and leave the background white.

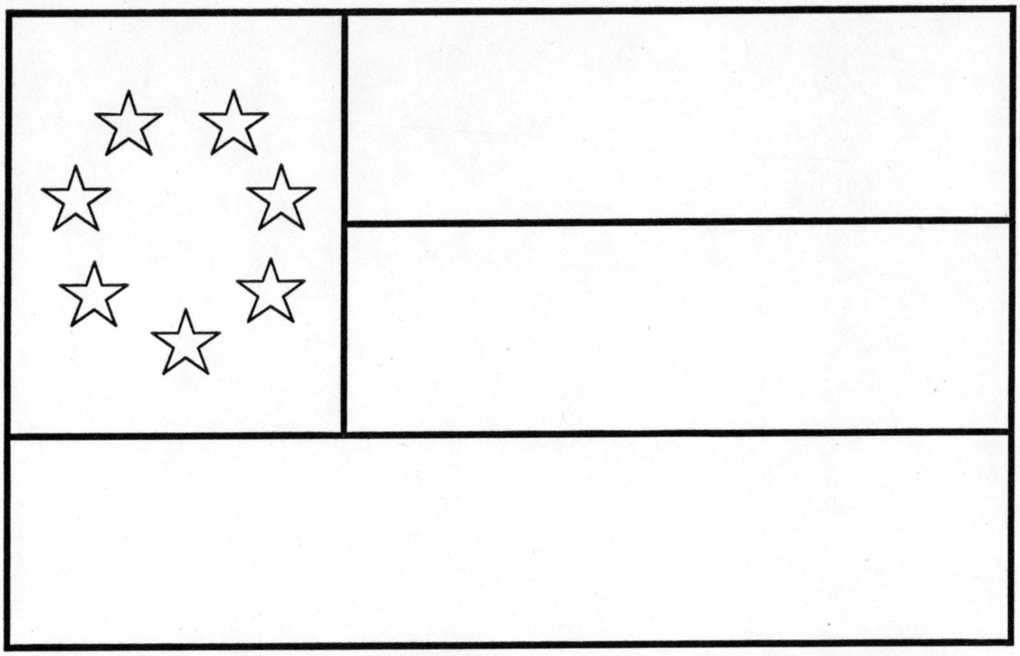

This is the official flag of the Confederacy which flew over Texas during the Civil War. The stars are white, and the background is blue. The top and bottom stripes are red and the middle stripe is white.

This is the official battle flag of the Confederacy. This flag was carried by many Texas troops during some of the most famous battles of the war. To color this flag, the middle of the "X" should be blue. The small border around the "X" and the stars should be white. The four triangular sections around the "X" should be red.

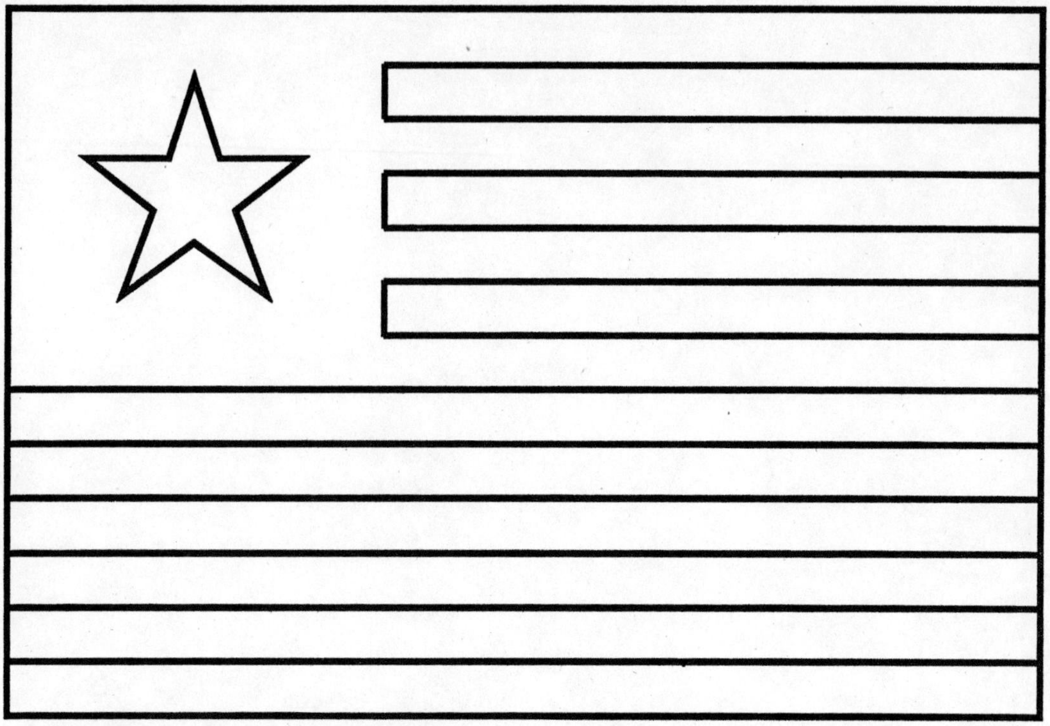

In 1819, Dr. James Long settled at Nacogdoches. When his wife had a baby, she became the "Mother of Texas" for having the first American child born in Texas. The star is white and the background is red. Color the stripes like those of the U.S. flag.

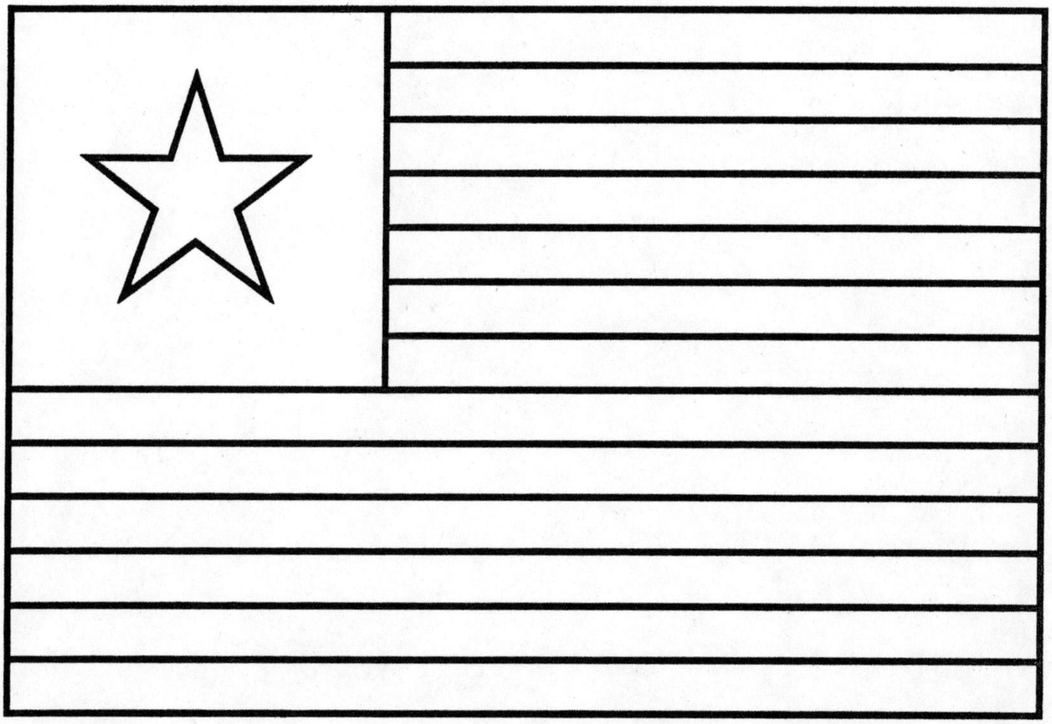

When Texas was a republic, there was an official Texas Navy and this was the flag used on the ships. The star is white and the background is blue. The stripes are like those of the U.S. flag.

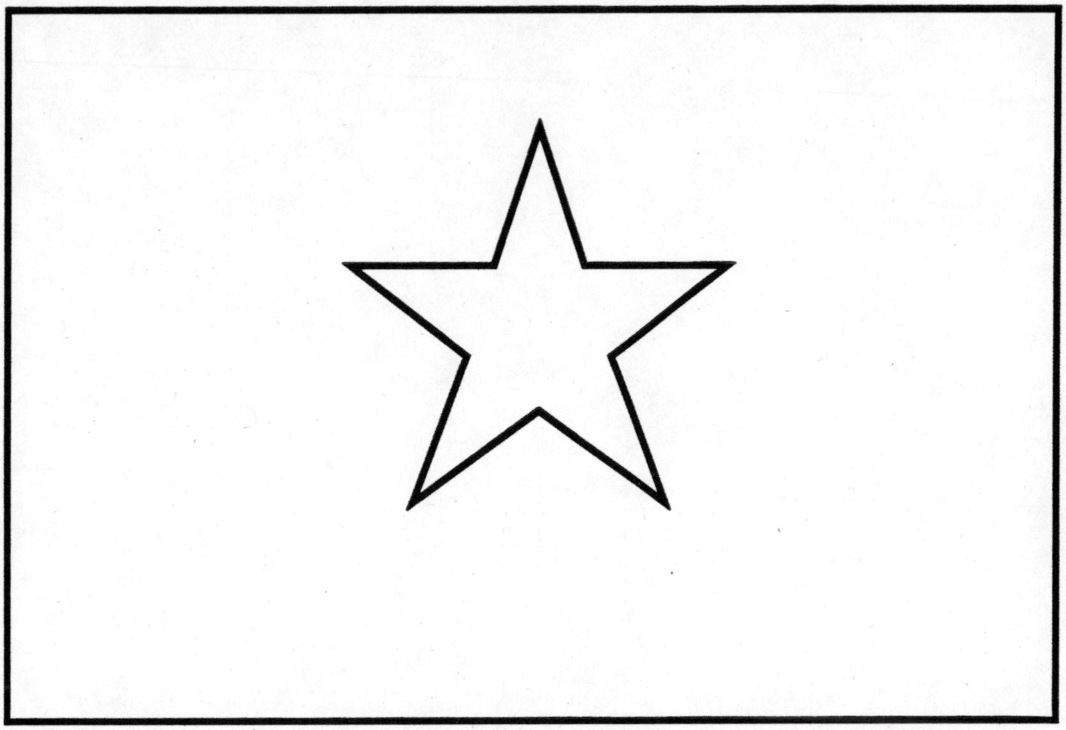

David G. Burnet, the first president of the Republic of Texas, was the man who suggested this flag. Adopted in 1836, Burnet's flag served as the official Texas banner until 1839. The background is blue and the star is gold.

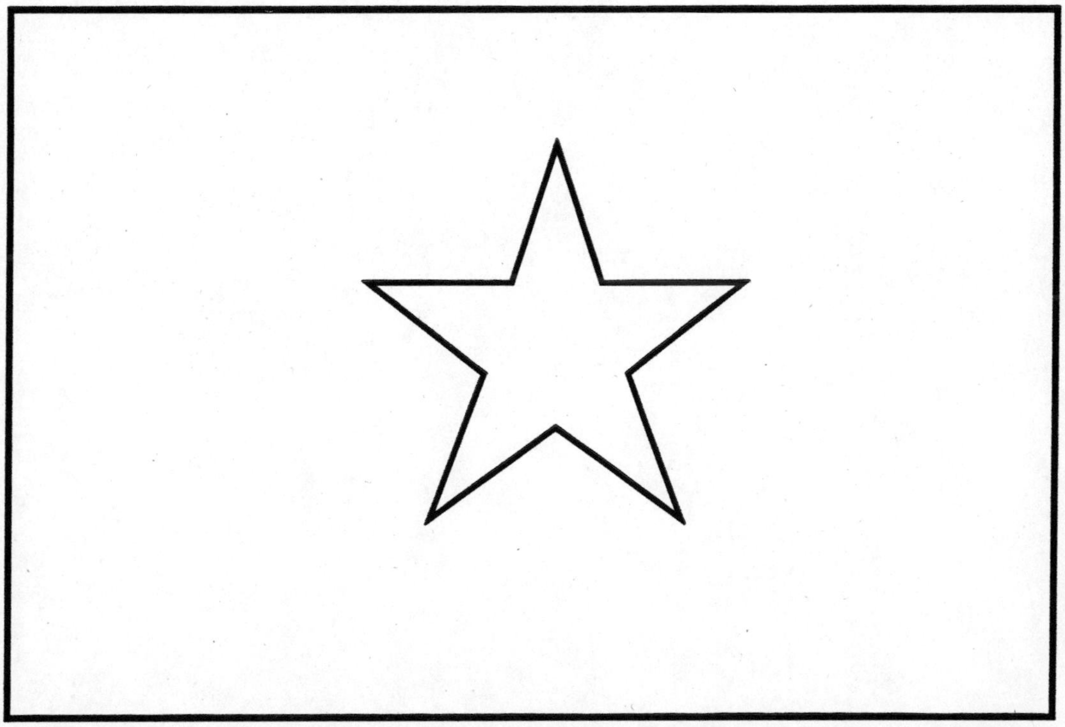

This flag, nicknamed "The Bonnie Blue Flag," was carried by the First Company of Texas Confederate Volunteers during the Civil War. Color the background blue and leave the star white.

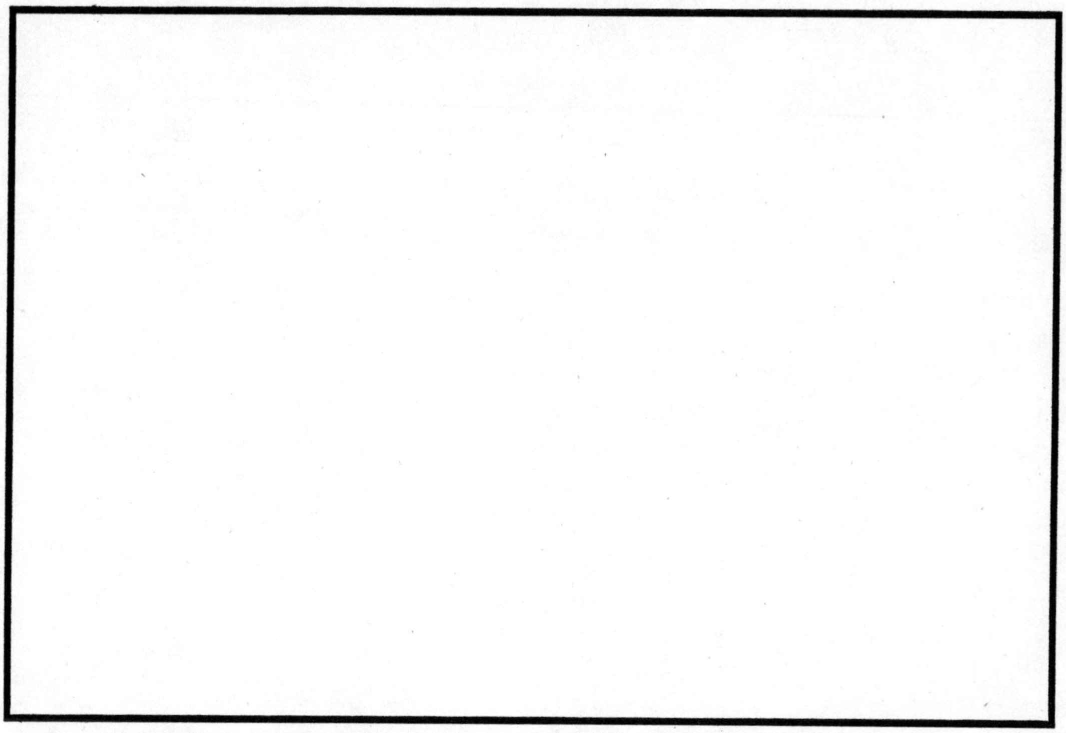

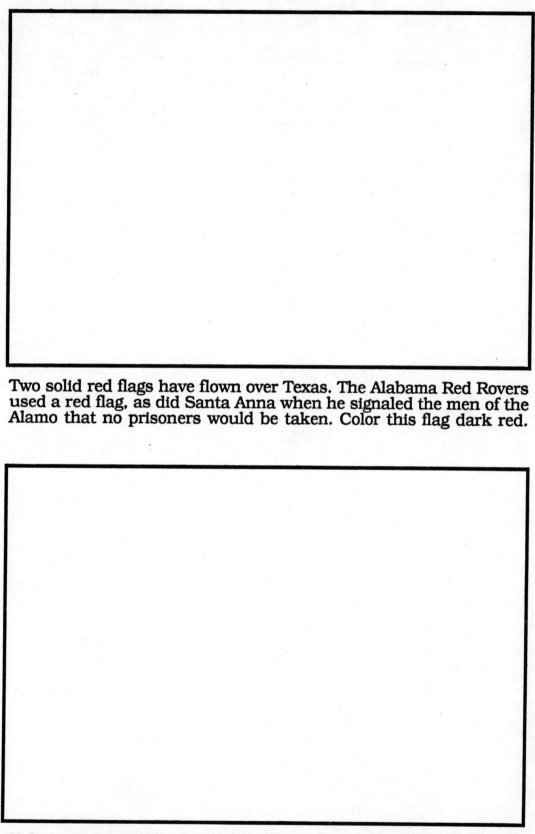

Two solid red flags have flown over Texas. The Alabama Red Rovers used a red flag, as did Santa Anna when he signaled the men of the Alamo that no prisoners would be taken. Color this flag dark red.

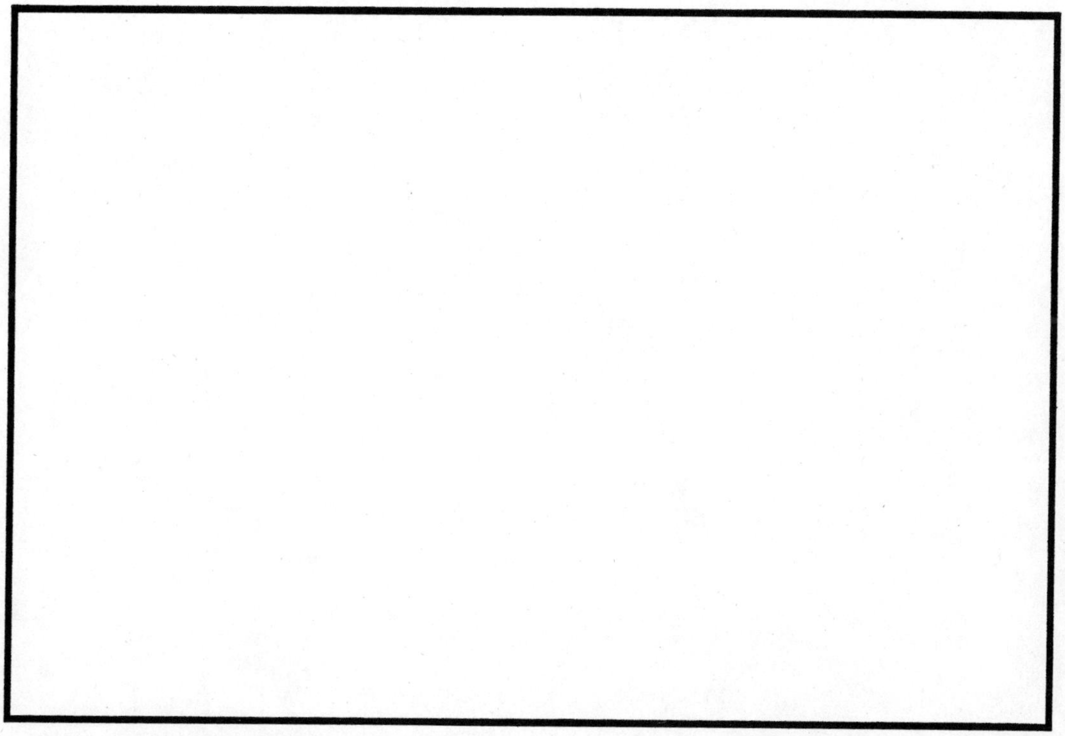

U.S. Army Lieutenant Augustus W. Magee used this flag when he and a small force tried to take control of Texas in 1813. The attempt failed. Color this flag a dark green.

TEXAS

Designed by General Lorenzo de Zavala, this was the first official flag of the Republic of Texas. This flag served until replaced by the flag designed by David Burnet. The background is blue and the star and letters are white.

LIBERTY or DEATH

One of the most famous Texas flags was this one designed by Johanna Troutman. It was carried by Ward's Georgia battalion during the Goliad campaign. The background is white and the star and letters are blue.

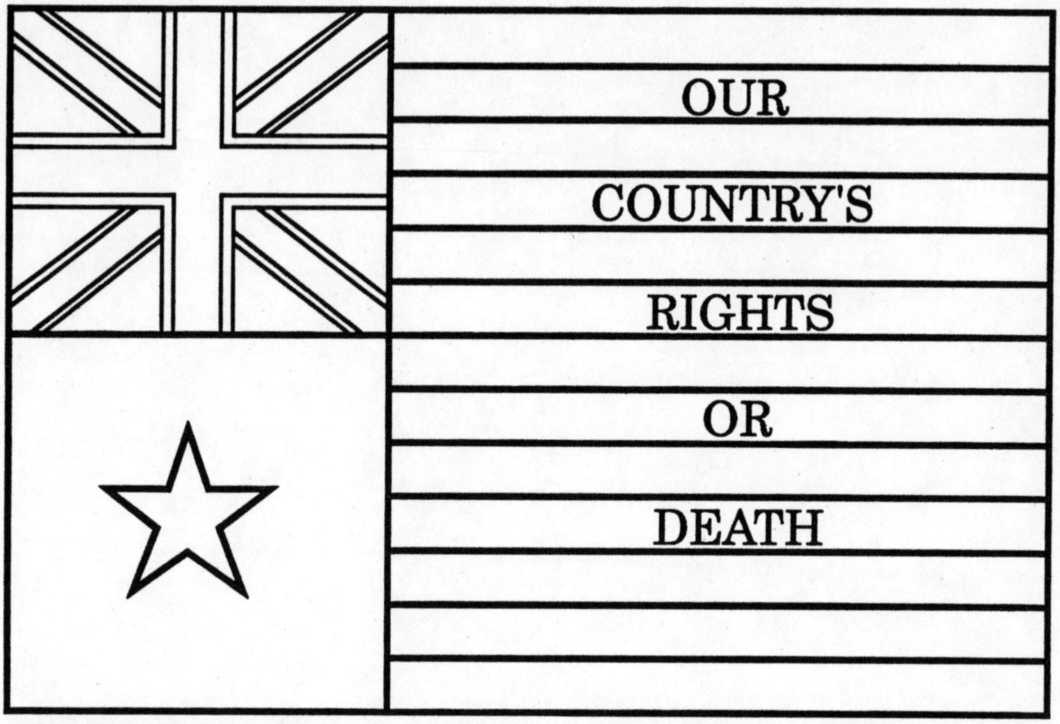
OUR
COUNTRY'S
RIGHTS
OR
DEATH

The San Felipe flag was used by Captain Moseley Baker during the Texas revolution. To color this flag, start in the upper left. The center of the stripes are red with the border white. The triangular portions are blue. In the lower left, the star is white and the background is green. Color the stripes on the right like the stripes on the U.S. flag.

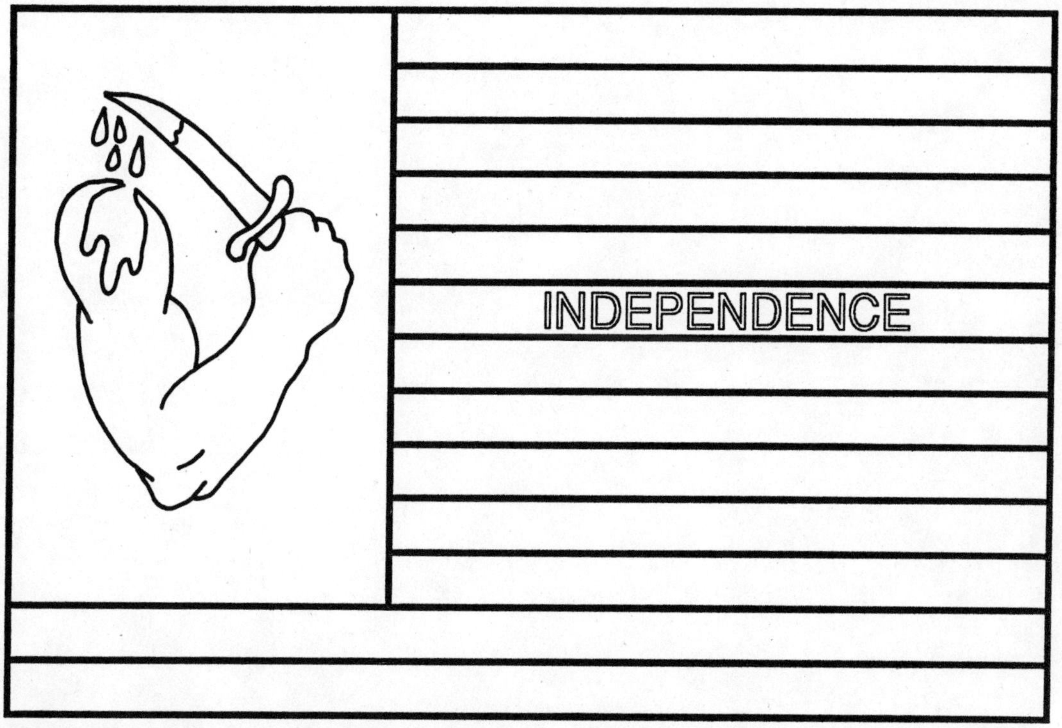
INDEPENDENCE

The "Bloody Flag" was carried by Captain William Brown at the siege of San Antonio during 1835. The background behind the arm is blue; the arm is white; the knife handle and blood on the arm and knife are red. The stripes are like those on the U.S. flag and "Independence" is red.

COME AND TAKE IT

When Mexican troops tried to get back a small cannon from the town of Gonzales, the Texans challenged them to "Come and Take it" and hoisted this flag. The Mexican troops withdrew without firing a shot and the town got to keep the cannon. The background is white. The star and letters are black. Do not color the cannon.

INDEPENDENCE

This flag, designed by Captain William Scott of Kentucky, was carried at the brief battle of Concepcion in 1835. The background is blue and the star and letters are white.

There were a lot of pirates along the Texas gulf coast in the early 1800s. This was the flag used by Don Louis de Aury in 1816. To color this flag, the outside border is red and the center is white. The top wreath is green and the sword and wheat branches are blue.

This Venezuelan flag was carried by the most famous Texas pirate of all time, Jean Lafitte. He used the flag while on Galveston Island between 1818 and 1821. The top stripe is yellow, the middle stripe is blue, and the bottom stripe is red.

Texas

Games

Texas Games

On the pages that follow you will find some fun and interesting games that you make and play. There are four games: a "Pecos Rodeo" game, a "Cards in the Hat" game, a "Help the Animals Across the Road" game, and finally the "Texas Oil Game."

To make the most of the games, you will have the best results if you glue or paste the boards onto poster board or cardboard for strength. Each game has some parts that you can color. Be sure, after you make each of the games, to put away all the supplies you used. And, remember the rule about always asking permission before starting any project in this book.

Each of the games has its own instructions. You will notice that each of the games can be played by several people, so why not invite some friends over? Also, the games are perfect for the entire family to play.

Let's RODEO

Let's RODEO

In 1883, the world's first rodeo was held in Pecos, Texas. Cowboys from several local ranches got together to see who was the best. They rode wild horses and bulls and showed what they could do with a rope. From that beginning, the sport of rodeo has become one of the most popular in the United States. Today, rodeo contestants travel all over the world to ride the bulls and the horses. Even though you can't do that right now, you can still have some fun with a special Pecos Rodeo game.

The Pecos Rodeo

General Instructions

Like a real rodeo, there are several events in this game. There are bull riding, bronc riding, bareback riding, steer wrestling, and barrel racing. To make the game easier to play, you may want to carefully remove each of the event pages so you can lay them flat on a table. As in a real rodeo, any number of people can play. This is a great game to play as a family.

For the bull riding, bronc riding, bareback riding, and steer wrestling events, you will need a regular deck of cards. Use only the face cards, the tens, and the joker to form your rodeo deck. If you do not have a joker, use an ace instead. This deck of 17 cards becomes your Pecos Rodeo card deck. You will use it in all the events except the barrel race.

Since bull riding, bronc riding, and bareback riding are timed events in a rodeo, you will use the cards to determine your time. You begin by turning over the top card and placing it in the proper space. Continue until you turn over the joker, which means your turn has ended. For bull riding, bronc riding, and bareback riding, your score will be found under the last card you placed before you turned the joker. Since real cowboys must ride for at least 8 seconds, you must turn over at least 8 cards for your turn to count. For these three events, you want the highest score possible. The longer you go before you turn the joker, the better your score will be.

In steer wrestling, you want the lowest possible time, but you must give the steer a head start. In this event, you want to turn the joker as quickly as possible after the first five cards have been turned. If the joker is one of the first five cards you turn, your score is a penalty time of 25 seconds.

For barrel racing, you will use one die (instead of a pair of dice) and a penny instead of your rodeo deck of cards. Each contestant moves around the course according to the number rolled on the die. The winner will complete the course in the lowest number of rolls.

In a real rodeo, there are usually many performances called go rounds. For each go round there is a winner and the contestant with the best total score for all go rounds is the event winner. In this game you can play as many go rounds as you like to make the game long or short.

On the back of each event page there is a Pecos Rodeo Tally Sheet that you will use to find the winner of each event and the best all-around cowboy. Before you begin to play, study the instructions on the next page so you will know how to keep score. There are six tally sheets. If you think you might want to play this game more then six times, you might ask a parent to make some copies of the tally sheet so you can use them for other games. If you don't get copies, you can always make your own talley sheet on any blank piece of paper. Good luck and have fun!

How to use the Rodeo Tally Sheet

In the Pecos Rodeo, like any rodeo, there are many winners. The rodeo talley sheet is used to determine each winner and it is really easy to use. The first winners are those cowboys who win each go round. To find out who those winners are, use the chart. For example, record all the bull riding scores for the first go round on the chart as in the example below:

Bull Riding	Cowboy No. 1	Cowboy No. 2	Cowboy No. 3	Cowboy No. 4	Cowboy No. 5
1st Go Round	75	0	65	55	0

The winner for the first go round in bull riding would be Cowboy No. 1 because he had the highest score. Remember, for bull riding, bronc riding, and bareback riding, the highest score is the winner. For steer wrestling and barrel racing, the lowest score is the winner. Each time a go round is completed, you can determine the individual winner.

When all go rounds are complete for each event, you can find out who is the champion for that particular event. After all the scores have been recorded, you must add them and put the total in the space provided, as in the example to the right. The cowboy with the highest total in bull riding, bronc riding, and bareback riding is the overall champion. The cowboy with the lowest total score for steer wrestling and barrel racing will be the winner for those events.

Bull Riding	Cowboy No. 1
1st Go Round	75
2nd Go Round	0
3rd Go Round	65
4th Go Round	75
Total Score	215

The winner for the entire rodeo will be the All-Around Champion cowboy. To find that champion, you will use the Grand Total section of the Pecos Rodeo Talley Sheet. In the spaces provided, write the total for each cowboy for each event. To learn each cowboy's grand total score, add the bull riding, bronc riding, and bareback riding and then subtract the steer racing and barrel racing. The cowboy with the highest total score will be the All-Around Champion and the winner of the Pecos Rodeo game!

Just for fun, use your math skills to find the winner in the example at right. See the answer in the back of the book to check your work.

Grand Totals for all Go Rounds.

Bull Riding	215	200	195	225	185
Bronc Riding +	175	215	185	210	225
Bareback +	205	165	235	200	175
Steer Wrestle -	57	63	55	95	85
Barrel Race -	80	75	70	90	65
Grand Total =					

Pecos Rodeo Tally Sheet

Bull Riding	Cowboy No. 1	Cowboy No. 2	Cowboy No. 3	Cowboy No. 4	Cowboy No. 5
1st Go Round					
2nd Go Round					
3rd Go Round					
4th Go Round					
Total Score					

Bronc Riding					
1st Go Round					
2nd Go Round					
3rd Go Round					
4th Go Round					
Total Score					

Bareback Riding					
1st Go Round					
2nd Go Round					
3rd Go Round					
4th Go Round					
Total Score					

Steer Wrestle	Cowboy No. 1	Cowboy No. 2	Cowboy No. 3	Cowboy No. 4	Cowboy No. 5
1st Go Round					
2nd Go Round					
3rd Go Round					
4th Go Round					
Total Score					

Barrel Race					
1st Go Round					
2nd Go Round					
3rd Go Round					
4th Go Round					
Total Score					

Grand Totals for all Go Rounds.

Bull Riding					
Bronc Riding +					
Bareback +					
Steer Wrestle -					
Barrel Race -					
Grand Total =					

Bull Riding

40 style points, 90 total score

35 style points, 85 total score

30 style points, 80 total score

25 style points, 75 total score

20 style points, 70 total score

15 style points, 65 total score

10 style points, 60 total score

5 style points, 55 total score

8-second ride, 50 points

7-second ride, no points

6-second ride, no points

5-second ride, no points

4-second ride, no points

3-second ride, no points

2-second ride, no points

Oops! You got thrown in the gate! No Points.

Place your cards face up to create a row of cards as shown.

Chute Number 1

Bull riding is one of the most dangerous events in any rodeo. Contestants must try to ride the bull while holding onto a small cinch with one hand. The contestant's other hand must not touch the bull in any way. To complete a ride, you must stay on the bull for 8 seconds. For a real cowboy, a bull ride is the longest 8 seconds of his life.

Shuffle your rodeo deck of cards and place them face down in this space.

To play, turn over the cards one at a time and place them face up to the left as shown. Continue until you turn the joker. Your score will be found under the top of the last card you turned before the joker. Each time you play, be sure to record your score on the rodeo tally sheet.

Pecos Rodeo Tally Sheet

Bull Riding	Cowboy No. 1	Cowboy No. 2	Cowboy No. 3	Cowboy No. 4	Cowboy No. 5
1st Go Round					
2nd Go Round					
3rd Go Round					
4th Go Round					
Total Score					

Bronc Riding					
1st Go Round					
2nd Go Round					
3rd Go Round					
4th Go Round					
Total Score					

Bareback Riding					
1st Go Round					
2nd Go Round					
3rd Go Round					
4th Go Round					
Total Score					

Steer Wrestle	Cowboy No. 1	Cowboy No. 2	Cowboy No. 3	Cowboy No. 4	Cowboy No. 5
1st Go Round					
2nd Go Round					
3rd Go Round					
4th Go Round					
Total Score					

Barrel Race					
1st Go Round					
2nd Go Round					
3rd Go Round					
4th Go Round					
Total Score					

Grand Totals for all Go Rounds.

Bull Riding					
Bronc Riding +					
Bareback +					
Steer Wrestle -					
Barrel Race -					
Grand Total =					

Bronc Riding

40 style points, 90 total score

35 style points, 85 total score

30 style points, 80 total score

25 style points, 75 total score

20 style points, 70 total score

15 style points, 65 total score

10 style points, 60 total score

5 style points, 55 total score

8-second ride, 50 points

7-second ride, no points

6-second ride, no points

5-second ride, no points

4-second ride, no points

3-second ride, no points

2-second ride, no points

Oops! You got thrown in the gate! No Points.

Place your cards face up to create a row of cards as shown.

Chute Number 2

In bronc riding, contestants ride wild horses while sitting in a saddle. You can hold on to the saddle horn with one hand but your other hand must not touch the horse or the saddle. For a complete ride, you must stay in the saddle for 8 seconds.

Shuffle your rodeo deck of cards and place them face down in this space.

To play, turn over the cards one at a time and place them face up to the left as shown. Continue until you turn the joker. Your score will be found under the top of the last card you turned before the joker. Each time you play, be sure to record your score on the rodeo tally sheet.

Pecos Rodeo Tally Sheet

Bull Riding	Cowboy No. 1	Cowboy No. 2	Cowboy No. 3	Cowboy No. 4	Cowboy No. 5
1st Go Round					
2nd Go Round					
3rd Go Round					
4th Go Round					
Total Score					

Bronc Riding	Cowboy No. 1	Cowboy No. 2	Cowboy No. 3	Cowboy No. 4	Cowboy No. 5
1st Go Round					
2nd Go Round					
3rd Go Round					
4th Go Round					
Total Score					

Bareback Riding	Cowboy No. 1	Cowboy No. 2	Cowboy No. 3	Cowboy No. 4	Cowboy No. 5
1st Go Round					
2nd Go Round					
3rd Go Round					
4th Go Round					
Total Score					

Steer Wrestle	Cowboy No. 1	Cowboy No. 2	Cowboy No. 3	Cowboy No. 4	Cowboy No. 5
1st Go Round					
2nd Go Round					
3rd Go Round					
4th Go Round					
Total Score					

Barrel Race	Cowboy No. 1	Cowboy No. 2	Cowboy No. 3	Cowboy No. 4	Cowboy No. 5
1st Go Round					
2nd Go Round					
3rd Go Round					
4th Go Round					
Total Score					

Grand Totals for all Go Rounds.

Bull Riding					
Bronc Riding +					
Bareback +					
Steer Wrestle -					
Barrel Race -					
Grand Total =					

Bareback Riding

40 style points, 90 total score

35 style points, 85 total score

30 style points, 80 total score

25 style points, 75 total score

20 style points, 70 total score

15 style points, 65 total score

10 style points, 60 total score

5 style points, 55 total score

8-second ride, 50 points

7-second ride, no points

6-second ride, no points

5-second ride, no points

4-second ride, no points

3-second ride, no points

2-second ride, no points

Oops! You got thrown in the gate! No Points.

Place your cards face up to create a row of cards as shown.

Chute Number 3

In bareback riding, contestants ride wild horses without using a saddle. You can hold on to a cinch around the horse with one hand but your other hand must not touch the horse in any way. For a complete ride, you must stay on the horse for 8 seconds.

Shuffle your rodeo deck of cards and place them face down in this space.

To play, turn over the cards one at a time and place them face up to the left as shown. Continue until you turn the joker. Your score will be found under the top of the **last** card you turned before the joker. Each time you play, be sure to record your score on the rodeo tally sheet.

Pecos Rodeo Tally Sheet

Bull Riding	Cowboy No. 1	Cowboy No. 2	Cowboy No. 3	Cowboy No. 4	Cowboy No. 5
1st Go Round					
2nd Go Round					
3rd Go Round					
4th Go Round					
Total Score					

Bronc Riding					
1st Go Round					
2nd Go Round					
3rd Go Round					
4th Go Round					
Total Score					

Bareback Riding					
1st Go Round					
2nd Go Round					
3rd Go Round					
4th Go Round					
Total Score					

Steer Wrestle	Cowboy No. 1	Cowboy No. 2	Cowboy No. 3	Cowboy No. 4	Cowboy No. 5
1st Go Round					
2nd Go Round					
3rd Go Round					
4th Go Round					
Total Score					

Barrel Race					
1st Go Round					
2nd Go Round					
3rd Go Round					
4th Go Round					
Total Score					

Grand Totals for all Go Rounds.

Bull Riding					
Bronc Riding +					
Bareback +					
Steer Wrestle -					
Barrel Race -					
Grand Total =					

Steer Wrestling

In steer wrestling, the object is to ride your horse beside a wild steer; jump off your horse and onto the steer; and then wrestle the steer to make it fall to the ground in the quickest possible time. Contestants must give the steer a small head start and then catch it as fast as they can. Having a fast, well-trained horse is very important. It is also smart not to jump onto the horns of the steer!

16-second time

15-second time

14-second time

13-second time

12-second time

11-second time

10-second time

9-second time

8-second time

7-second time

6-second time

25-second penalty score

25-second penalty score

25-second penalty score

25-second penalty score

Oops! You did not give the poor steer enough of a head start. 25 seconds is your score.

Place your cards face up to create a row of cards as shown.

Shute Number 4

Shuffle your rodeo deck of cards and place them face down in this space.

To play, turn over the cards one at a time and place them face up to the left as shown. Continue until you turn the joker. Your score will be found under the top of the last card you turned before the joker. Each time you play, be sure to record your score on the rodeo tally sheet.

Pecos Rodeo Tally Sheet

Bull Riding	Cowboy No. 1	Cowboy No. 2	Cowboy No. 3	Cowboy No. 4	Cowboy No. 5
1st Go Round					
2nd Go Round					
3rd Go Round					
4th Go Round					
Total Score					

Bronc Riding	Cowboy No. 1	Cowboy No. 2	Cowboy No. 3	Cowboy No. 4	Cowboy No. 5
1st Go Round					
2nd Go Round					
3rd Go Round					
4th Go Round					
Total Score					

Bareback Riding	Cowboy No. 1	Cowboy No. 2	Cowboy No. 3	Cowboy No. 4	Cowboy No. 5
1st Go Round					
2nd Go Round					
3rd Go Round					
4th Go Round					
Total Score					

Steer Wrestle	Cowboy No. 1	Cowboy No. 2	Cowboy No. 3	Cowboy No. 4	Cowboy No. 5
1st Go Round					
2nd Go Round					
3rd Go Round					
4th Go Round					
Total Score					

Barrel Race	Cowboy No. 1	Cowboy No. 2	Cowboy No. 3	Cowboy No. 4	Cowboy No. 5
1st Go Round					
2nd Go Round					
3rd Go Round					
4th Go Round					
Total Score					

Grand Totals for all Go Rounds.

Bull Riding					
Bronc Riding +					
Bareback +					
Steer Wrestle -					
Barrel Race -					
Grand Total =					

The Pecos Barrel Race

In a real barrel race, the object is to ride a horse around each of the three barrels and make it back to the finish line in the least amount of time. To play this event in the Pecos rodeo, you will need one die (instead of a pair of dice) and a penny so you can mark your progress.

Roll the die and move the penny the number of spaces equal to the die roll. Continue until you have crossed the finish line. Each roll of the die counts as one second. The number of rolls it takes you to cross the finish line will be your event time. The contestant who gets the lowest time wins.

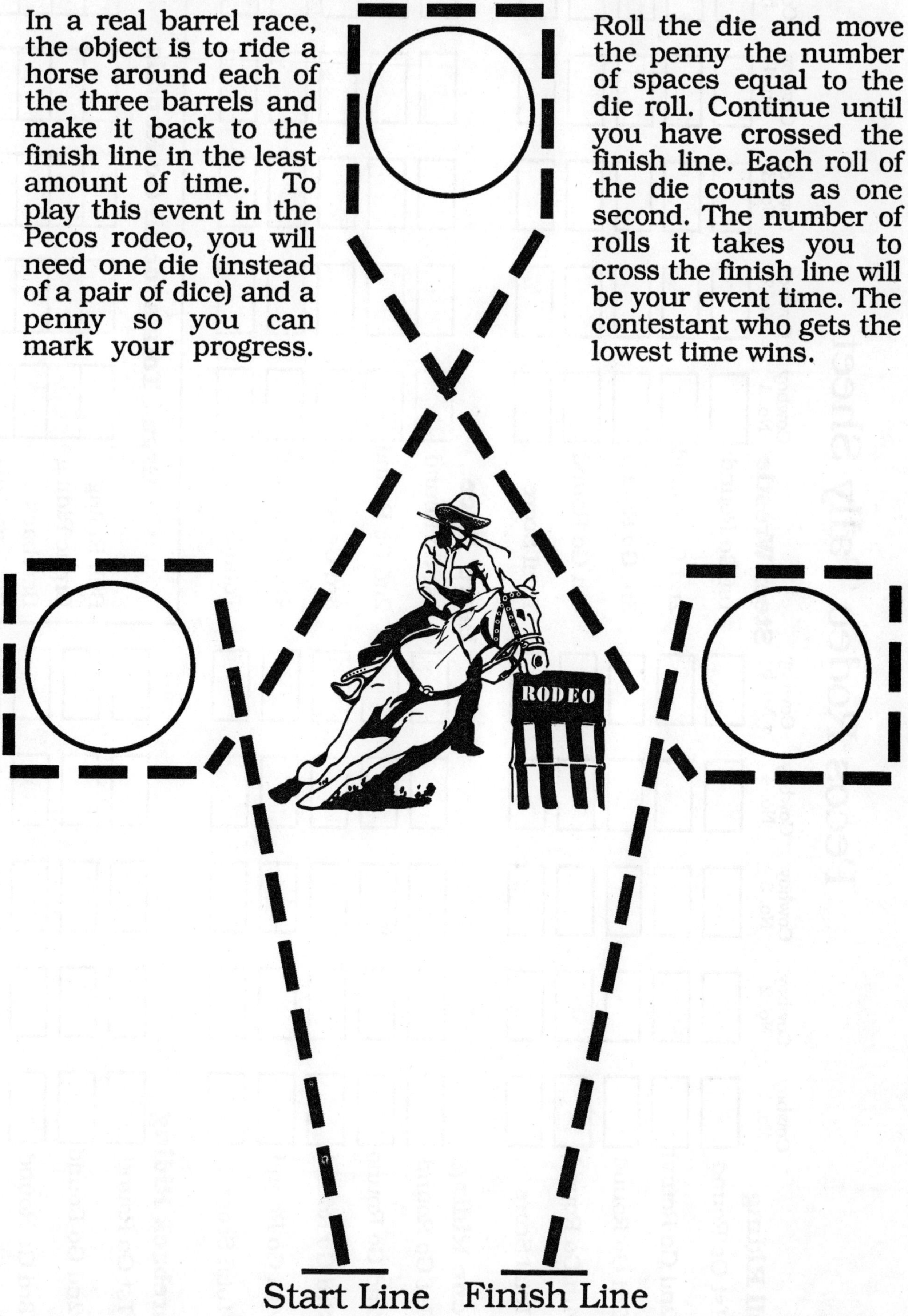
RODEO
Start Line
Finish Line

Pecos Rodeo Tally Sheet

Bull Riding	Cowboy No. 1	Cowboy No. 2	Cowboy No. 3	Cowboy No. 4	Cowboy No. 5
1st Go Round					
2nd Go Round					
3rd Go Round					
4th Go Round					
Total Score					

Bronc Riding					
1st Go Round					
2nd Go Round					
3rd Go Round					
4th Go Round					
Total Score					

Bareback Riding					
1st Go Round					
2nd Go Round					
3rd Go Round					
4th Go Round					
Total Score					

Steer Wrestle	Cowboy No. 1	Cowboy No. 2	Cowboy No. 3	Cowboy No. 4	Cowboy No. 5
1st Go Round					
2nd Go Round					
3rd Go Round					
4th Go Round					
Total Score					

Barrel Race					
1st Go Round					
2nd Go Round					
3rd Go Round					
4th Go Round					
Total Score					

Grand Totals for all Go Rounds.

Bull Riding					
Bronc Riding +					
Bareback +					
Steer Wrestle -					
Barrel Race -					
Grand Total =					

The Cards in the Hat Game

After a hard day of riding and roping in a rodeo, cowboys are often very tired. To relax, many of them sit around camp and toss cards into a hat. It is a simple game that you can play and have lots of fun.

To play the game, you will need a full deck of cards and a cowboy hat. If you don't have a cowboy hat, use any other hat. If you don't have any hat at all, use a small cardboard box.

Place the hat top down (open side up) and step back about four paces. Sit down in a chair or on the floor and then try to toss each of the cards into the hat one at a time. Each card that goes completely into the hat counts five points. Cards that land on the rim of the hat or on the floor do not count. When you have thrown the entire deck, count the number of cards in the hat to determine your score. If you are playing against a friend, let the friend have a turn to see who gets the highest score.

10
J
Q
K
A

Hint: When you try this game, you will learn that cards tend to fly in all directions when thrown because they are so thin. Try flipping the cards at different angles to make them curve into the hat. Also, do not throw too hard or you will not have much luck.

Suggestion: This is a great game for the entire family. Why not practice a little and then challenge the members of your family to a contest.

Please Remember: After playing this game, you should put away the cards and the hat where they belong. Thanks, partner.

Help the Animals Across the Road Game

As you know, sometimes it is very difficult for small animals to make it across the wide, modern highways. Well, here's your chance to help some animals and have a great time with a game you made for yourself. Just follow the instructions on the next page to make the game. Get ready for some fun!

Instructions for making the game

Step one: Carefully remove all the pages with the road panels, the median, and the game pieces.
Step two: Glue the median on a large piece of poster board.
Step three: Glue the top of road panel 1 to the median as indicated.
Step four: Glue the bottom of road panel 2 to the median as indicated. This completes your game board. Color it if you like.
Step five: Cut out the game pieces and glue them to scrap pieces of poster board for strength. Color each piece a different color.
Step six: Carefully remove the game card pages and then cut out each individual card. For strength, glue the pages to poster board before cutting out each piece.
That's it: Now you are ready to play!

Your game board should look like this.

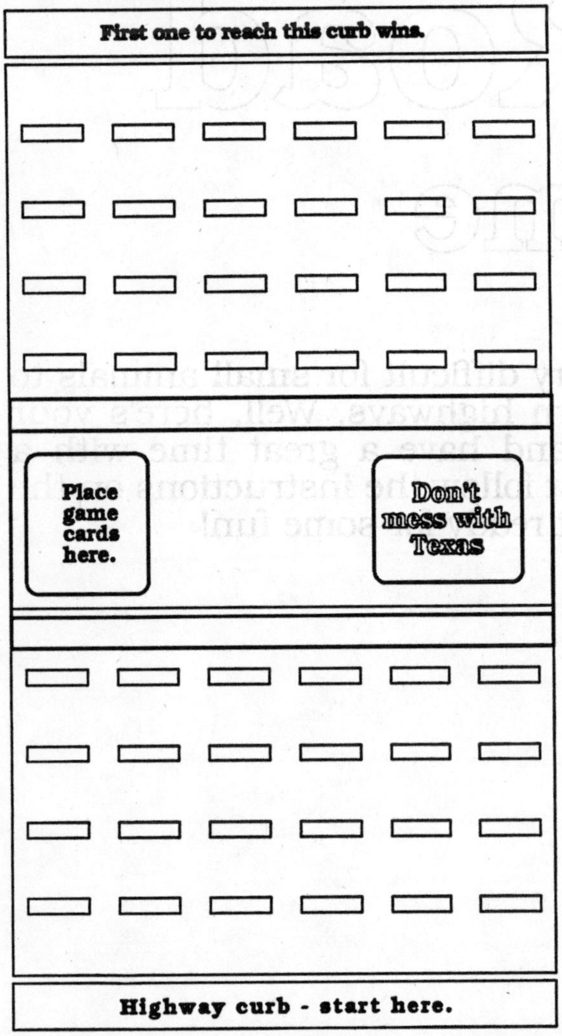
First one to reach this curb wins.
Place game cards here.
Don't mess with Texas
Highway curb - start here.

How to play the game.

This game can be played by up to four people or more if you make teams.

To play, first mix up the game cards well and then place them in a stack on the space in the road median.

Decide which player will go first. That person draws a game card, follows the instructions, and then puts the card back on the bottom of the pile. The game then continues with each person taking a turn until someone crosses the entire road.

Remember, the median counts as one lane so do not just jump over it.

To play by yourself, follow the same instructions but count to see how many turns it takes to reach the other side. Then continue playing to see if you can beat your record.

Remember! When you finish making the game, put away your supplies. When you finish playing the game, be sure to put it away in a safe place. You will have it to play with on another day.

Help the Animals Across the Road - panel 1.

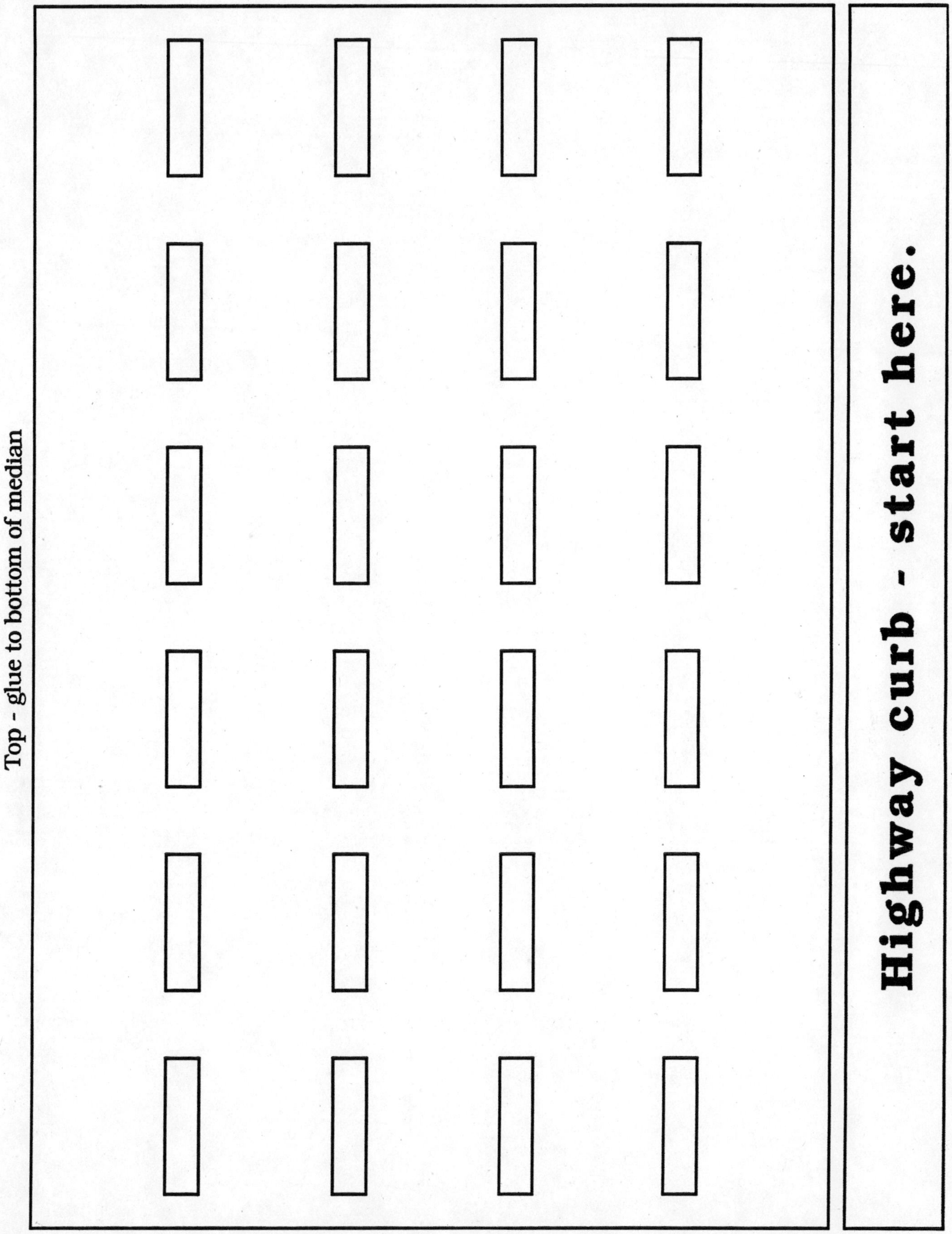
Top - glue to bottom of median
Highway curb - start here.

Color the highway a light gray. The stripes can be either white or yellow.

Help the Animals Across the Road - panel 2.

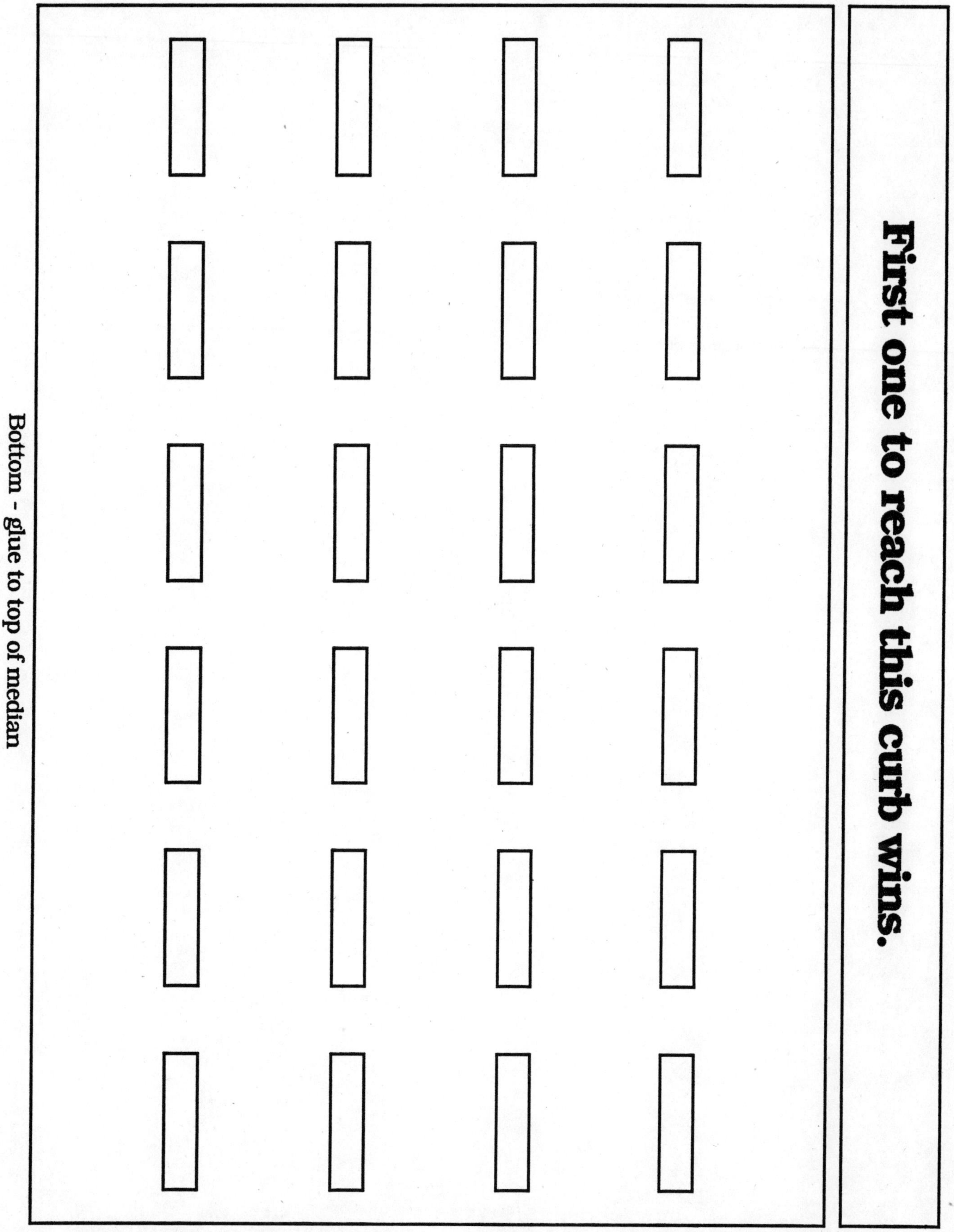
Bottom - glue to top of median
First one to reach this curb wins.

Color the highway a light gray. The stripes can be either white or yellow.

Help the Animals Across the Road - median

Game pieces

Median top - glue the bottom of panel 2 here.

Don't mess with Texas

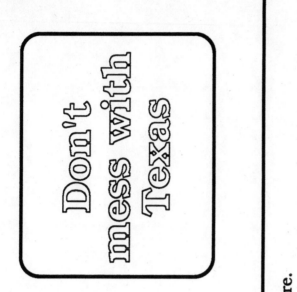

Place game cards here.

Median bottom - glue the top of panel 1 here.

Color the center portion green. Don't Mess With Texas should be blue letters and a white background.

All Clear! Move ahead one lane.	**All Clear!** Move ahead one lane.	**All Clear!** Move ahead two lanes.
All Clear! Move ahead one lane.	**All Clear!** Move ahead one lane.	**All Clear!** Move ahead two lanes.
All Clear! Move ahead one lane.	**All Clear!** Move ahead two lanes.	**All Clear!** Move ahead three lanes.
All Clear! Move ahead one lane.	**All Clear!** Move ahead two lanes.	**All Clear!** Move ahead three lanes.

Start Over! The road is too hot to cross.	**Wet pavement!** Slip back one lane.	**Getting Dark!** Go ahead one lane.
It's starting to rain. Miss one turn and dry off.	**Dry pavement.** Go ahead one lane.	**Lucky You!** Go ahead one lane.
Stop to rest. Miss one turn!	**You messed with Texas!** Go back one lane.	**You are stuck in road tar.** Miss one turn.
Glass on the road! Go to the median, either forward or backward.	**Someone messed with Texas.** Pick up the litter, move one lane, and then draw again for being a good Texan.	**Leap frog special!** Jump ahead two lanes!

Watch out! A motorcycle is coming. Go back one lane.	**Watch out!** A motorcycle is coming. Go back one lane.	**Watch out!** A car is coming. Go back one lane.
Watch out! A motorcycle is coming. Go back one lane.	**Watch out!** A motorcycle is coming. Go back one lane.	**Watch out!** A car is coming. Go back one lane.
Watch out! A motorcycle is coming. Go back one lane.	**Watch out!** A car is coming. Go back one lane.	**Watch out!** A big truck is coming. Go back one lane.
Watch out! A motorcycle is coming. Go back one lane.	**Watch out!** A car is coming. Go back one lane.	**Watch out!** A big truck is coming. Go back one lane.

Texas Oil Game

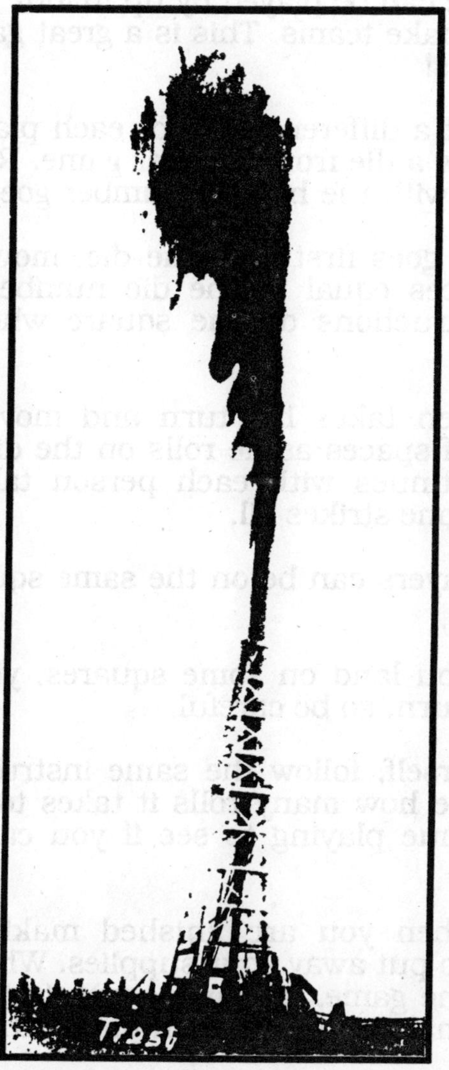
Trost

On January 10, 1901, Mr. A. F. Lucas discovered a vast oil field at a place called Spindletop, near Beaumont, Texas. It was the largest oil discovery in the world at the time. Suddenly, there was so much oil that it became cheap to convert (or refine) oil into gasoline that could be used in cars. As a result, Texas was responsible for all of us being able to ride around in cars instead of on horses! A lot of people have become rich drilling for oil, but a lot more have gone broke when they struck a dry hole.

In recent years, the price of oil has gone up and down a lot, which makes drilling a very large gamble. However, you can drill for oil by making the Texas Oil Game on the following pages. All you have to do is follow the instructions and have fun!

At left is the famous F. J. Trost picture of the great Lucas oil gusher. Used with the permission of the Barker Texas History Center at the University of Texas in Austin.

Texas Oil Game Assembly Instructions.

Step one: Carefully remove each of the following pages labeled Texas Oil Game panels and cut out each panel.
Step two: Using a full sheet of poster board, glue game panel 1 to the top left corner of the board.
Step three: Glue the top of panel 2 to the bottom of panel 1 as indicated. Then continue to glue all the panels in place. When you run out of room, start a new column.
Note: This is a very long gameboard, so you will fill up almost an entire piece of poster board. When all the panels are glued in place, cut the poster board into sections that can be taped together to complete the game. Be sure to ask your parents for help if you need it.
Step four: Once the board is complete, color the different layers. Some layers have designs to color and others are blank so you can make your own special designs.
Step five: Since drilling for oil costs a lot of money, use coins for playing pieces. Each player will use a different coin such as a penny, a nickel, a dime, or a quarter. **That's it.** Now you are ready to play the game.

Two assembled game panels

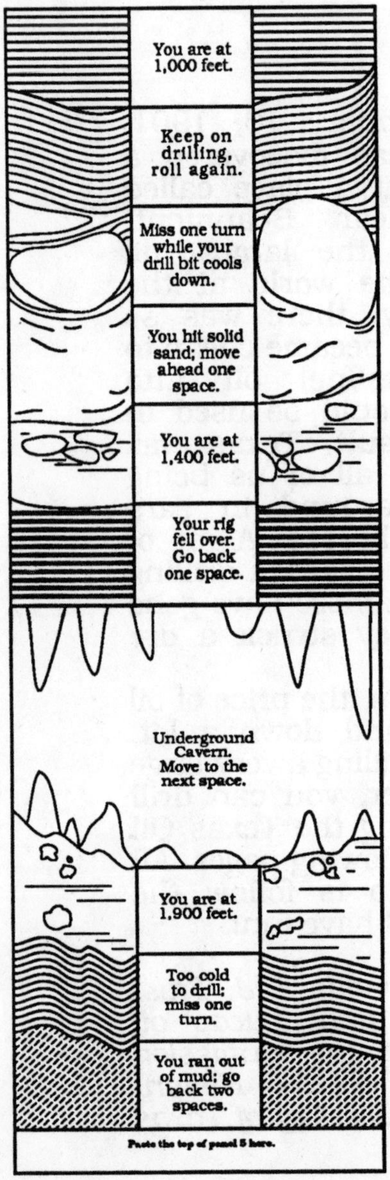

You are at 1,000 feet.
Keep on drilling, roll again.
Miss one turn while your drill bit cools down.
You hit solid sand; move ahead one space.
You are at 1,400 feet.
Your rig fell over. Go back one space.
Underground Cavern. Move to the next space.
You are at 1,900 feet.
Too cold to drill; miss one turn.
You ran out of mud; go back two spaces.
Paste the top of panel 5 here.

How to play the game - it's easy!

This Texas game can be played by up to four people or more if you make teams. This is a great game to play with parents!

To play, first get a different coin for each player or team and borrow a die from another game. Roll the die. The person with the highest number goes first.

The player who goes first rolls the die, moves the number of spaces equal to the die number, and follows the instructions on the square where he lands.

Each player then takes his turn and moves the same number of spaces as he rolls on the die. The game then continues with each person taking a turn until someone strikes oil.

Two or more players can be on the same square at the same time.

Remember, if you land on some squares, you will have to miss a turn, so be careful.

To play by yourself, follow the same instructions, but count to see how many rolls it takes to strike oil. Then continue playing to see if you can beat your record.

Remember! When you are finished making the game, be sure to put away your supplies. When you finish playing the game, be sure to put it in a safe place. You will have it to play with on another day.

Texas Oil Game, Panel 1.

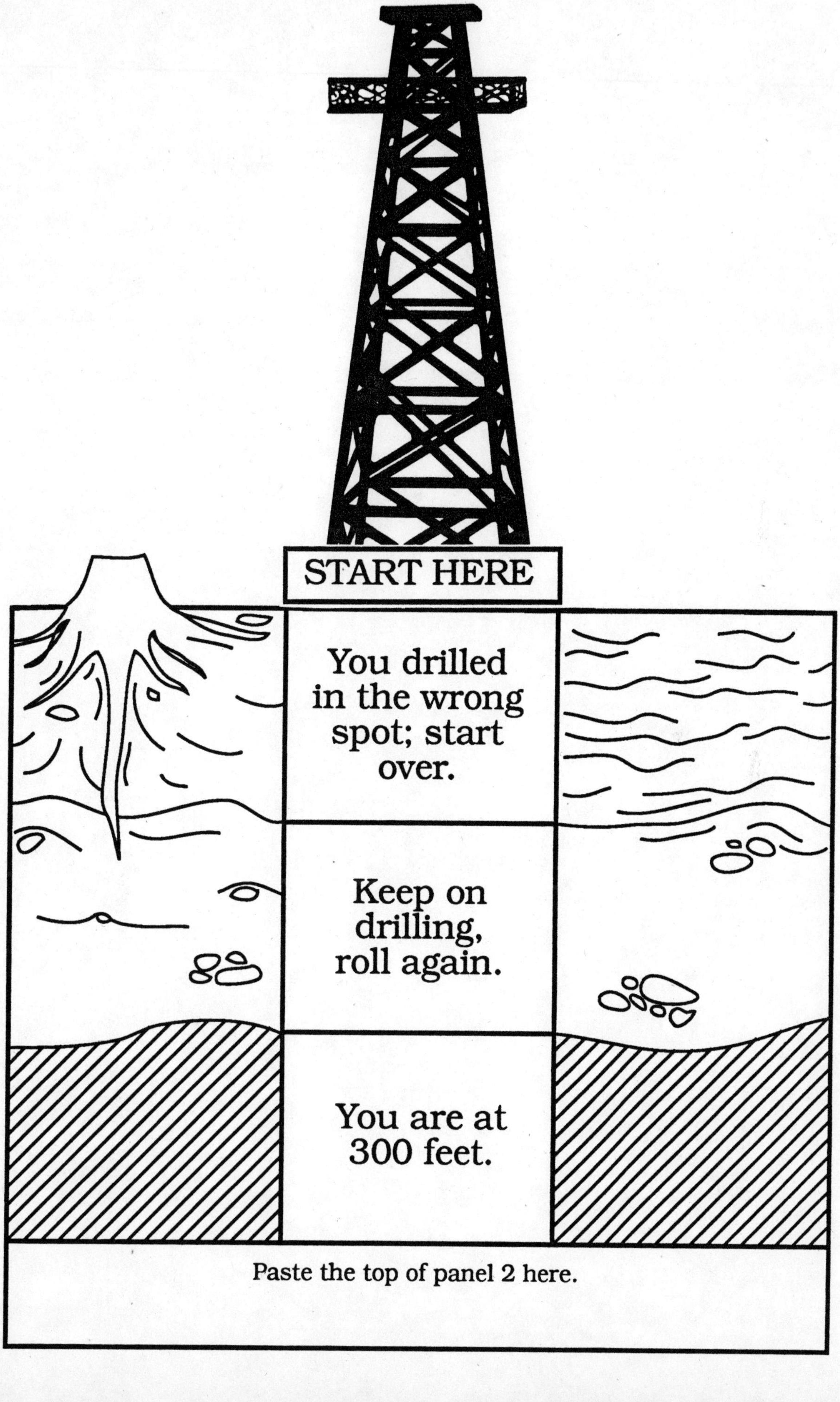
START HERE
You drilled in the wrong spot; start over.
Keep on drilling, roll again.
You are at 300 feet.
Paste the top of panel 2 here.

Texas Oil Game, Panel 2.

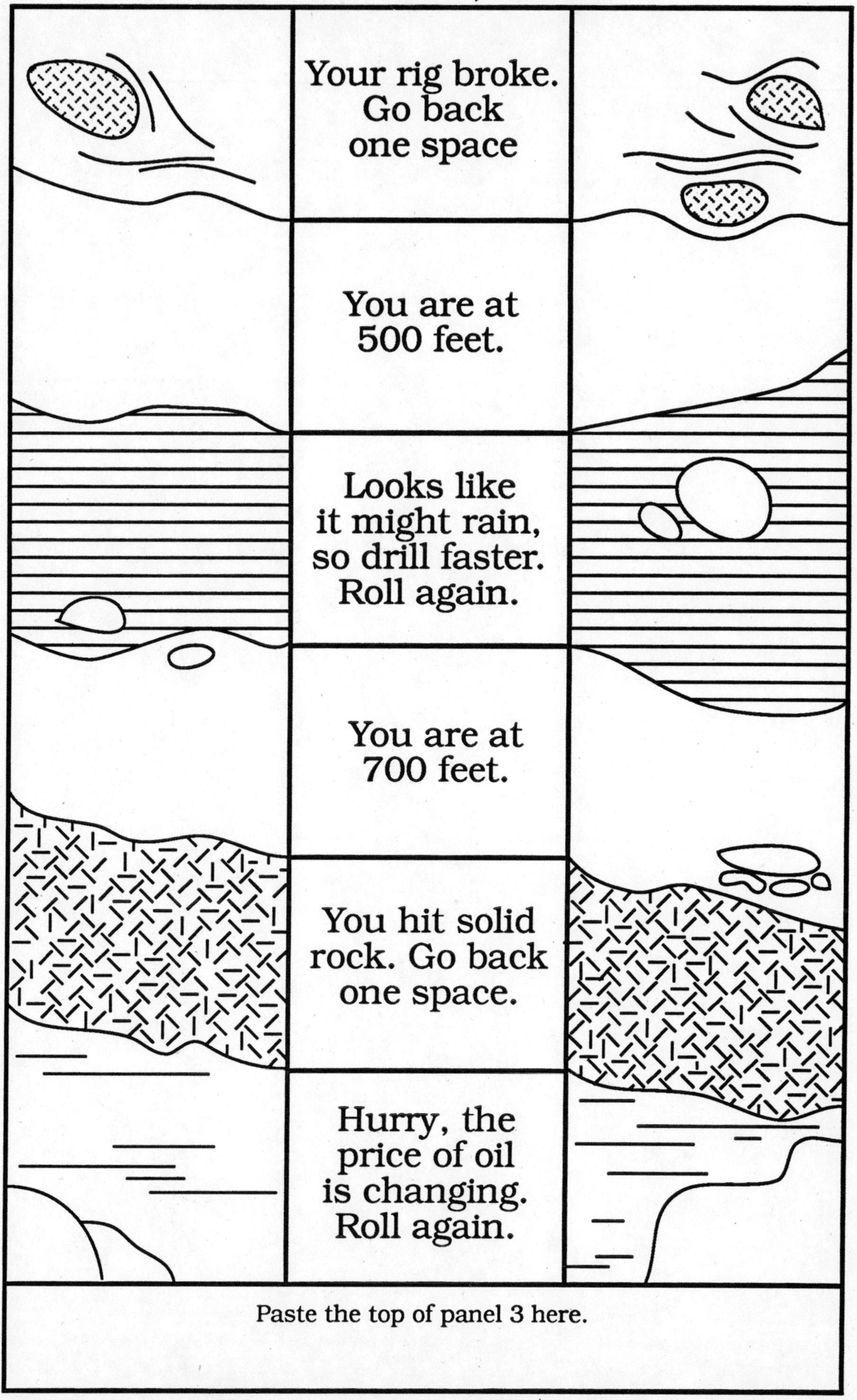
Your rig broke. Go back one space
You are at 500 feet.
Looks like it might rain, so drill faster. Roll again.
You are at 700 feet.
You hit solid rock. Go back one space.
Hurry, the price of oil is changing. Roll again.
Paste the top of panel 3 here.

Texas Oil Game, Panel 3.

You are at 1,000 feet.
Keep on drilling, roll again.
Miss one turn while your drill bit cools down.
You hit solid sand; move ahead one space.
You are at 1,400 feet.
Your rig fell over. Go back one space.
Paste the top of panel 4 here.

Texas Oil Game, Panel 4.

Underground Cavern. Move to the next space.
You are at 1,900 feet.
Too cold to drill; miss one turn.
You ran out of mud; go back two spaces.
Paste the top of panel 5 here.

Texas Oil Game, Panel 5.

You are at 2,200 feet.
Go to the bank for more money. Miss one turn.
You hit an underground stream. Go to the next space and miss one turn.
You are at 2,600 feet.
You are almost halfway. Roll again.
Paste the top of panel 6 here.

Texas Oil Game, Panel 6.

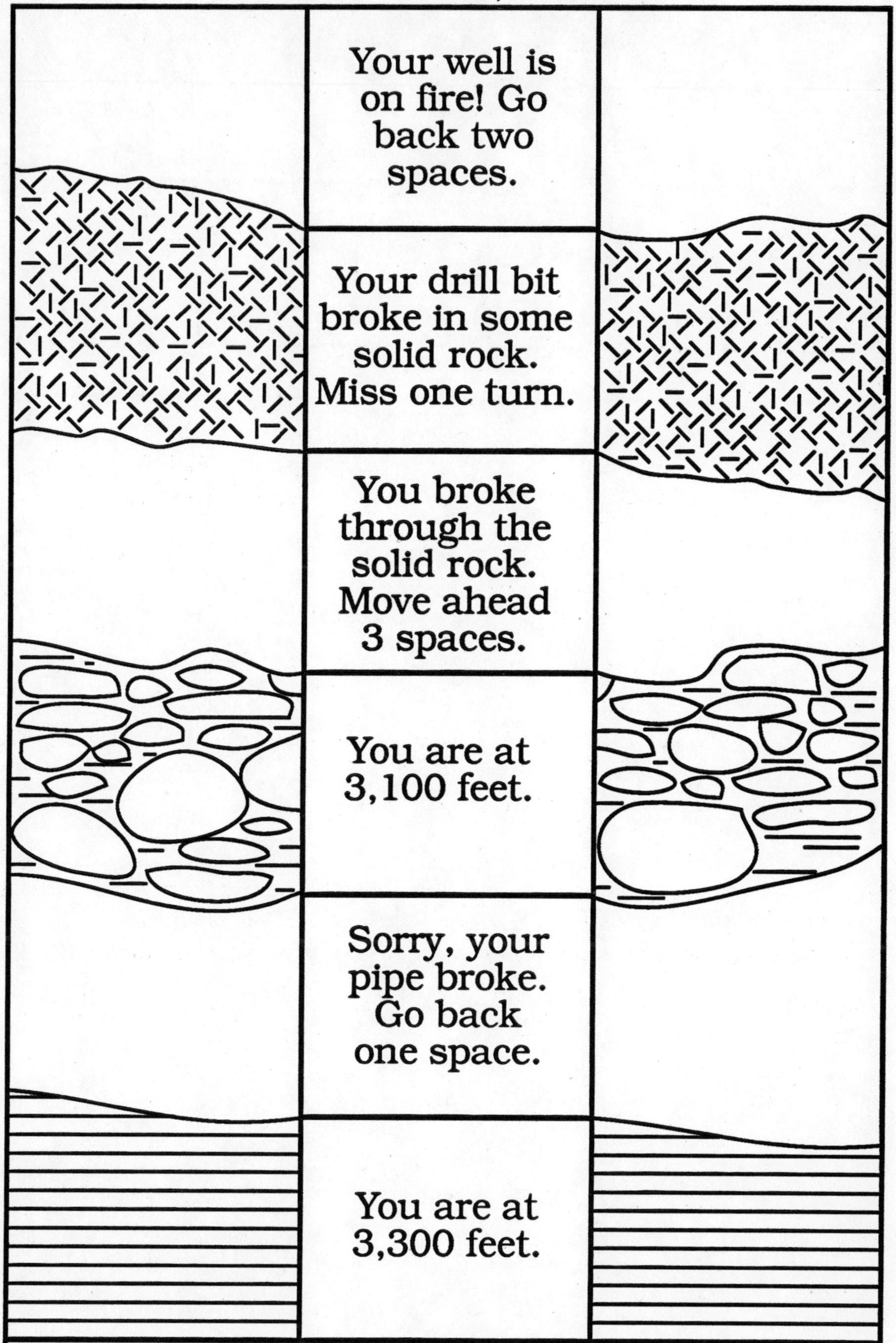
Your well is on fire! Go back two spaces.
Your drill bit broke in some solid rock. Miss one turn.
You broke through the solid rock. Move ahead 3 spaces.
You are at 3,100 feet.
Sorry, your pipe broke. Go back one space.
You are at 3,300 feet.

Paste the top of panel 7 here.

Texas Oil Game, Panel 7.

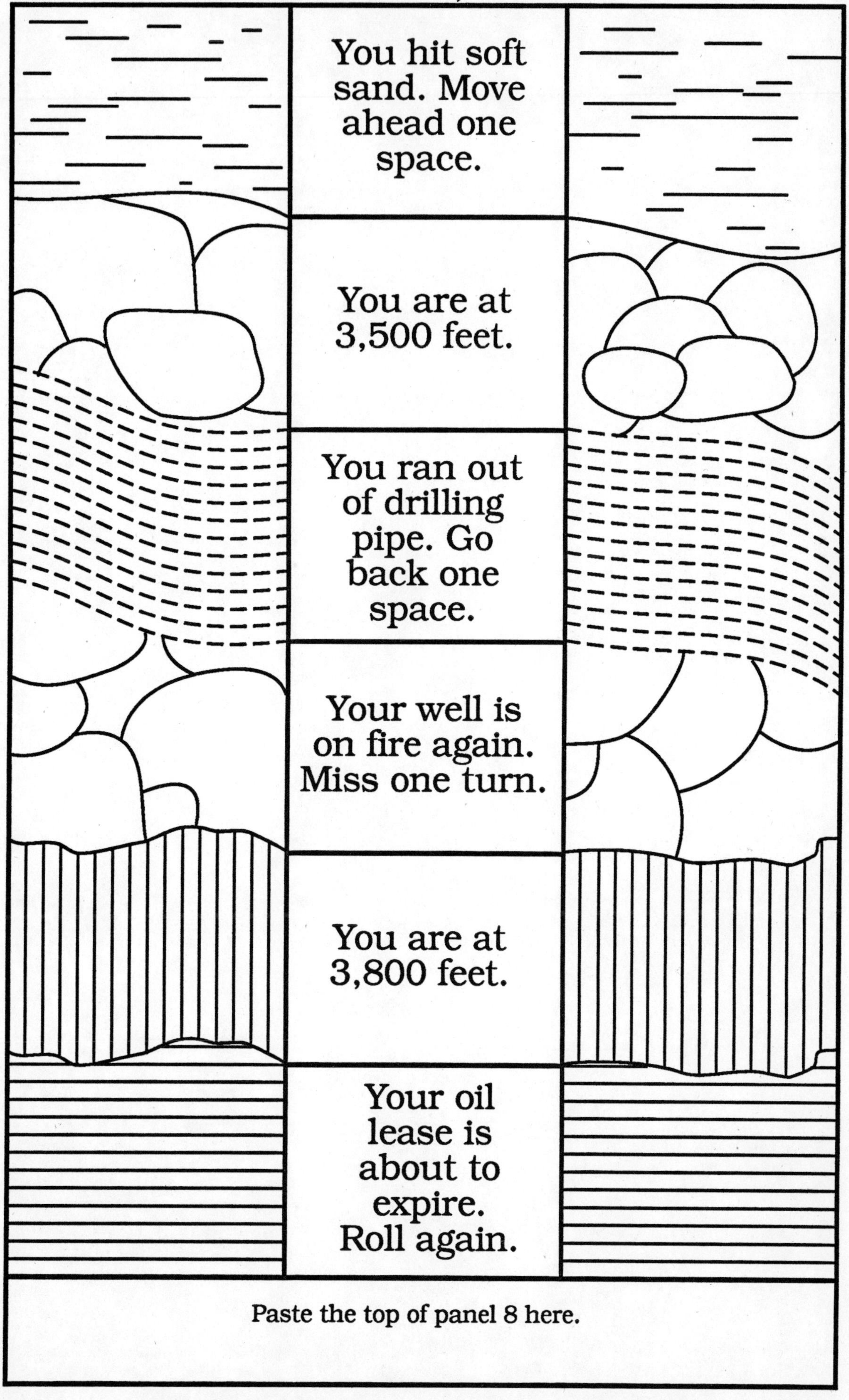
You hit soft sand. Move ahead one space.
You are at 3,500 feet.
You ran out of drilling pipe. Go back one space.
Your well is on fire again. Miss one turn.
You are at 3,800 feet.
Your oil lease is about to expire. Roll again.
Paste the top of panel 8 here.

Texas Oil Game, Panel 8.

You're doing great. Roll again.

Your well is full of mud. Miss one turn.

You are at 4,200 feet.

Your drill bit melted. Go back one space.

You hit gas and it blew your drill bit back two spaces.

You have a new drill bit. Roll again.

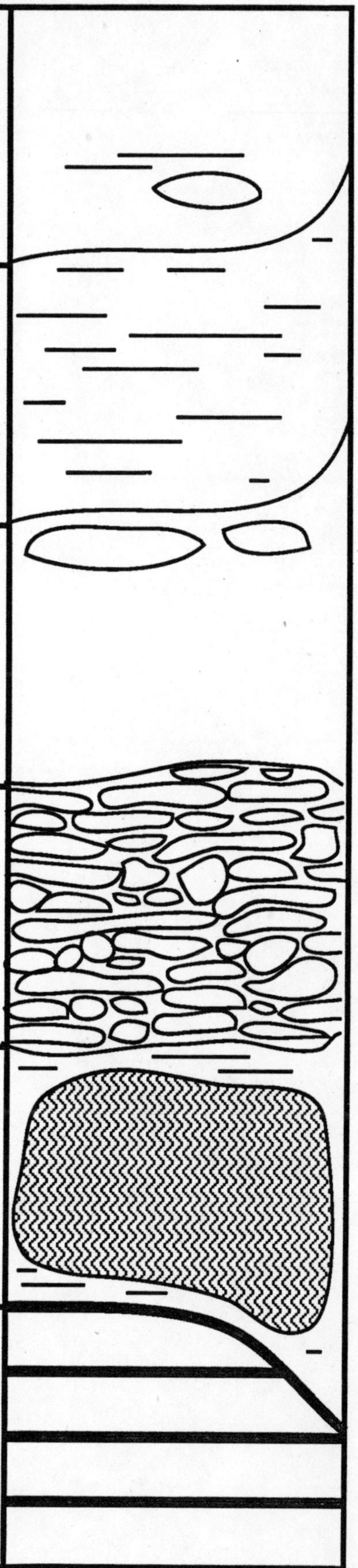

Paste the top of panel 9 here.

Texas Oil Game, Panel 9.

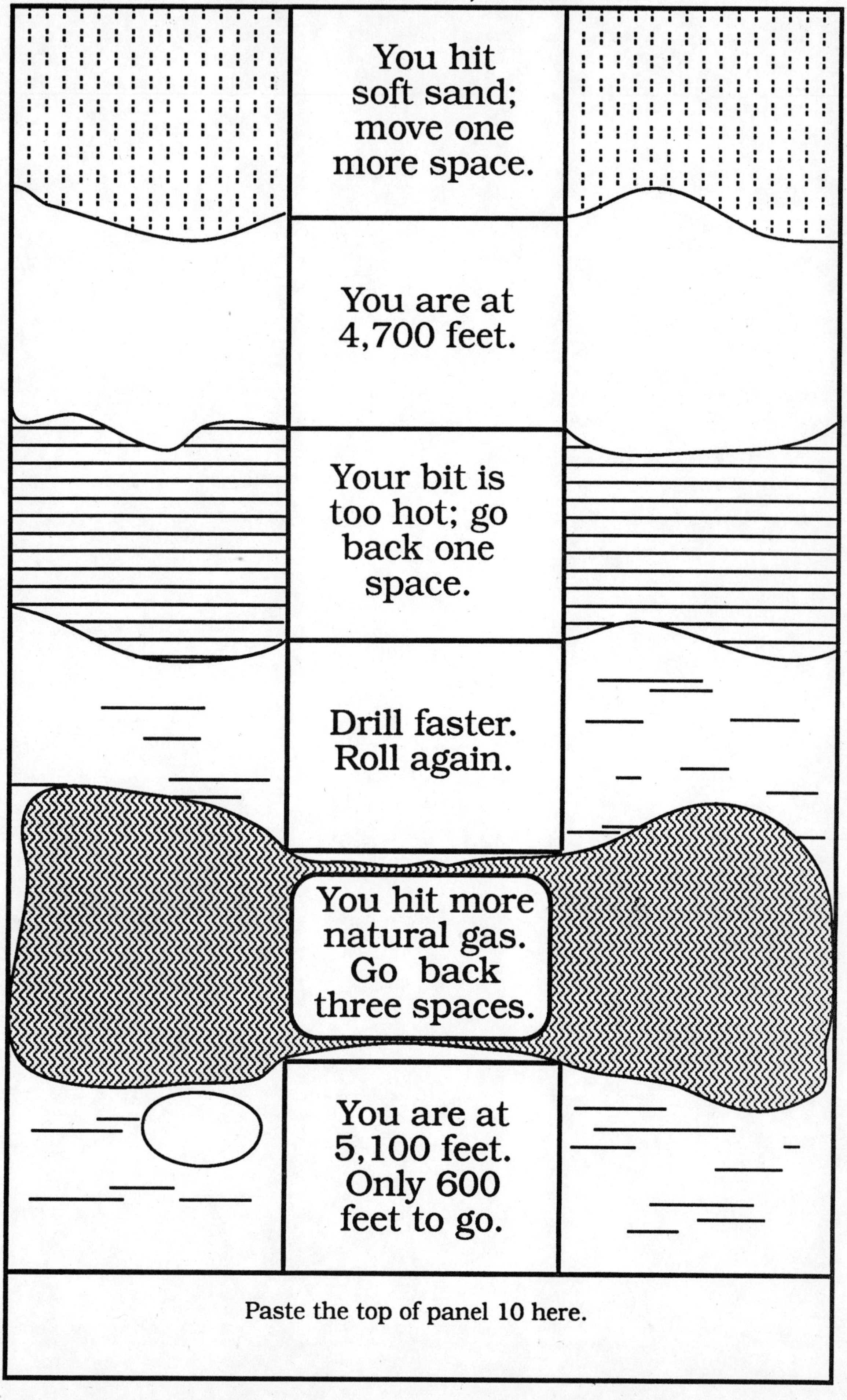
You hit soft sand; move one more space.
You are at 4,700 feet.
Your bit is too hot; go back one space.
Drill faster. Roll again.
You hit more natural gas. Go back three spaces.
You are at 5,100 feet. Only 600 feet to go.
Paste the top of panel 10 here.

Texas Oil Game, Panel 10.

Your pipe is bent; go back one space.
You are at 5,300 feet. Roll a 4 next time and win.
Oh, no! Your bit is too dull. Miss one turn to sharpen it.
Getting Close. Roll a 2 next time and win.
You hit oil sand. Miss one turn while you have it checked.
Congratulations! You struck oil at 5,600 feet.

Texas

Challenges

Texas Challenges

OK, here are some Texas challenges for you to try to solve. On the pages that follow, you will be challenged to find missing words and to make words. You will have the chance to show what you know about Texas stars, Texas sports teams, and the symbols of the state.

You will also have the opportunity to learn how to make and read cattle brands. Then you can test your knowledge with a special brand-reading challenge.

The challenges you will find are perfect to work by yourself. If you want to challenge your friends or parents, have them write their answers on a separate piece of paper. When everyone has finished all the challenges, you will find the answers in the back of the book. Good luck!

Texas Alphabet Soup

Can you supply the missing letter in each of the following sentences? Each time you know a letter, color that letter in the alphabet. If you find all the missing letters, each letter in the alphabet will be colored when you finish. If you use a different color for each letter, when they are all colored, you will have a rainbow of an alphabet. Good Luck!

A B C D E F G H I J K L M

N O P Q R S T U V W X Y Z

1. Stephen _. Austin is called the "Father of Texas."
2. The _ I T Ranch was once the largest in the world.
3. Today, the _ing Ranch is the largest in Texas.
4. Davy _rockett was a famous frontiersman who died at the Alamo.
5. _uana Parker was the greatest Comanche chief of all time.
6. Te_as is the Spanish spelling for Texas.
7. The word Amarillo is Indian for _ellow.
8. Old _apata is a town in South Texas that had to be moved for a lake.
9. Texas is the "Lone _tar State."
10. The Texas declaration of independence was signed in _ashington, Texas.
11. The state of Texas has been _nder six flags.
12. The _argemouth bass is the most popular fish in Texas.
13. _ ASA is the space headquarters in Houston, Texas.
14. _om Landry was once coach of the Dallas Cowboys.
15. Cowboys ride bulls in a rode_.
16. San Antonio, Texas is known for having many _issions.
17. The Apache _ndians once roamed through much of Texas.
18. Lyndon _. Johnson was once president of the United States.
19. The _avis Mountains are in far West Texas.
20. The _rmadillo is a famous Texas animal.
21. Pancho _illa was a famous Mexican bandit.
22. The Texas _angers are the most famous lawmen in the world.
23. The _orned toad, which is really a lizard, is an endangered species.
24. A lot of _ine trees grow in the forests of East Texas.
25. In Luckenbach, Texas, "_verybody is somebody."
26. Ruby Red is a type of grapefruit grown in the Rio _rande valley.

Texas Sports Challenge

How well do you know your Texas sports teams? Here's a challenge to test your knowledge. First, answer the questions below. Then, try to determine where each answer fits in the Texas Sports Challenge on the opposite page. Be careful when putting names in the puzzle because they might go up or down, forward or backward. The solution is in the back of the book.

1. The Texas **LONGHORNS** play football in Austin.
2. The SMU _ _ _ _ _ _ _ _ play football in Dallas.
3. The M_ _ _ _ _ _ _ _ _ play basketball in Dallas.
4. The Houston _ _ _ _ _ _ play football in the Astrodome.
5. The Texas Tech _ _ _ _ _ _ _ _ _ _ are from Lubbock.
6. The _ _ _ _ _ _ _ _ _ _ play indoor soccer in Dallas.
7. The _ _ _ _ _ hoop it up in San Antonio.
8. The players from Texas A&M are _ _ _ _ _ _.
9. The Rice _ _ _ _ do not sleep in trees.
10. The Houston _ _ _ _ _ _ _ play basketball.
11. _ _ _ Landry is now in the NFL Hall of Fame.
12. _ _ _ Phillips once coached the Houston Oilers.
13. The Texas _ _ _ _ _ _ _ play baseball in Arlington.
14. The _ _ _ _ _ _ _ _ _ _ _ were once in the Southwest Conference.
15. The TCU _ _ _ _ _ _ _ _ _ _ _ are purple.
16. The Baylor _ _ _ _ _ don't hug opponents.
17. The Houston _ _ _ _ _ _ _ are not scared kittens.
18. Jerry Jones now owns the Dallas _ _ _ _ _ _ _.
19. The Houston _ _ _ _ _ _ play indoor baseball.

Texas Sports Challenge

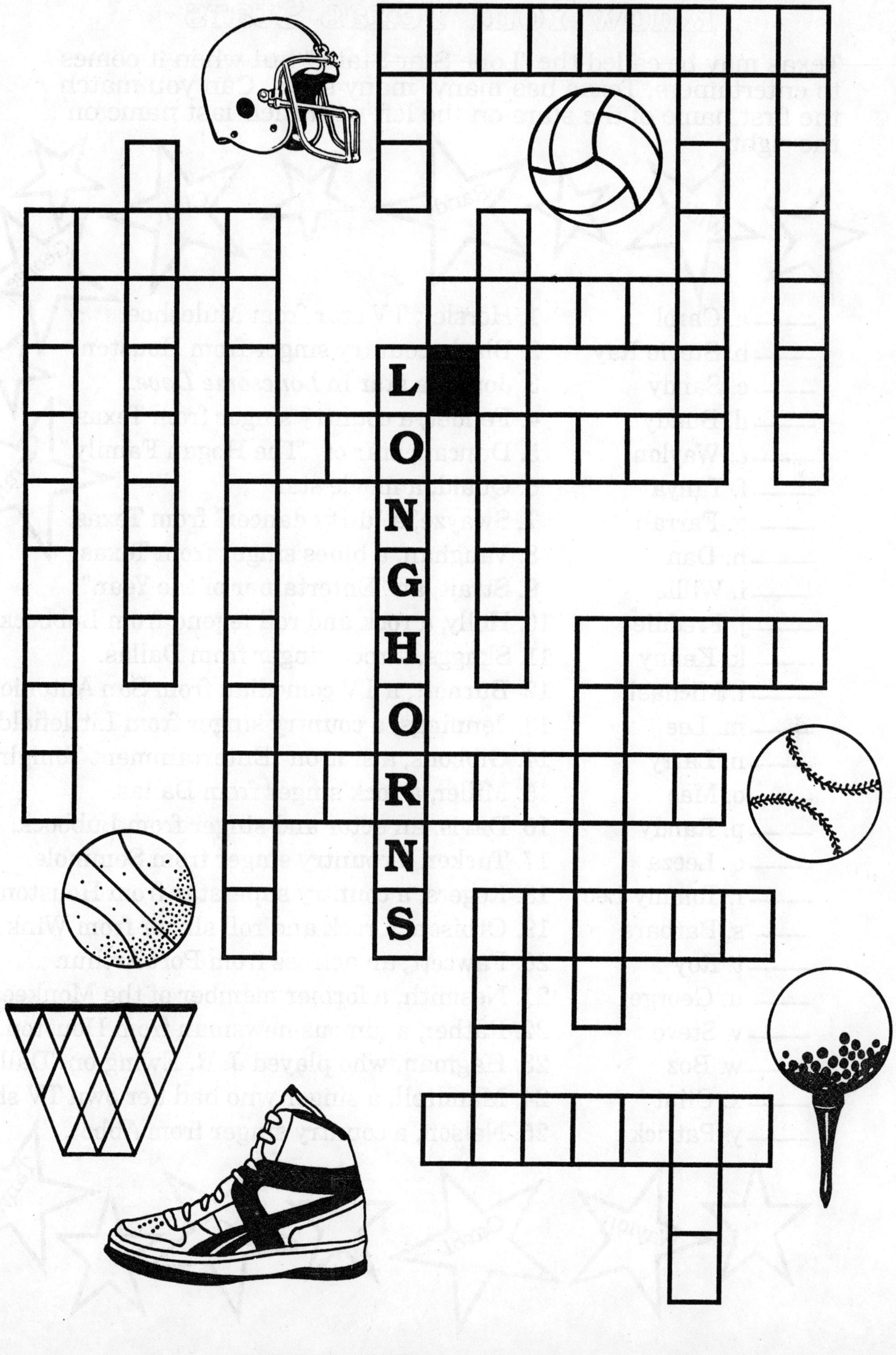
LONGHORNS

Texas Challenge . . .

Know Your Texas Stars

Texas may be called the "Lone Star State," but when it comes to entertainers, Texas has many, many stars. Can you match the first name of the stars on the left with their last name on the right?

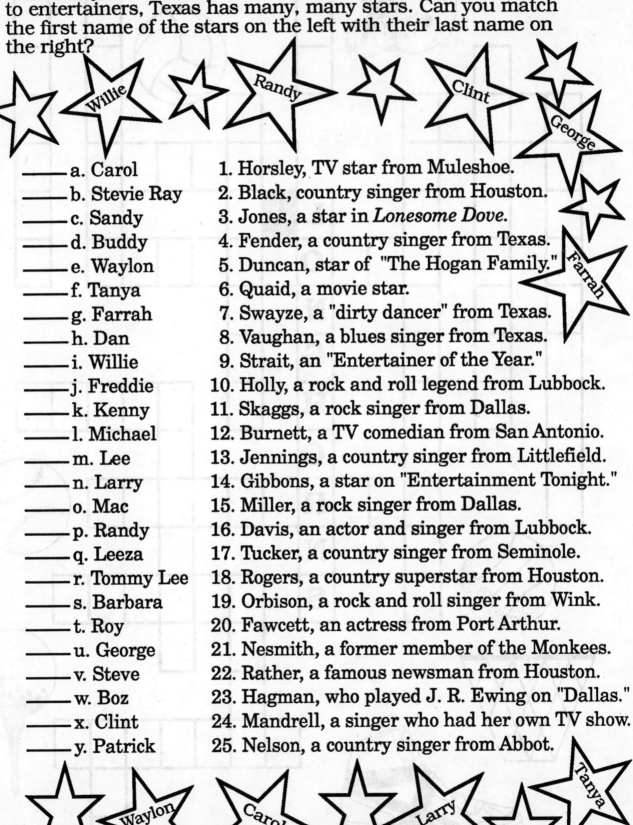

Willie
Randy
Clint
George

____ a. Carol	1. Horsley, TV star from Muleshoe.
____ b. Stevie Ray	2. Black, country singer from Houston.
____ c. Sandy	3. Jones, a star in *Lonesome Dove.*
____ d. Buddy	4. Fender, a country singer from Texas.
____ e. Waylon	5. Duncan, star of "The Hogan Family."
____ f. Tanya	6. Quaid, a movie star.
____ g. Farrah	7. Swayze, a "dirty dancer" from Texas.
____ h. Dan	8. Vaughan, a blues singer from Texas.
____ i. Willie	9. Strait, an "Entertainer of the Year."
____ j. Freddie	10. Holly, a rock and roll legend from Lubbock.
____ k. Kenny	11. Skaggs, a rock singer from Dallas.
____ l. Michael	12. Burnett, a TV comedian from San Antonio.
____ m. Lee	13. Jennings, a country singer from Littlefield.
____ n. Larry	14. Gibbons, a star on "Entertainment Tonight."
____ o. Mac	15. Miller, a rock singer from Dallas.
____ p. Randy	16. Davis, an actor and singer from Lubbock.
____ q. Leeza	17. Tucker, a country singer from Seminole.
____ r. Tommy Lee	18. Rogers, a country superstar from Houston.
____ s. Barbara	19. Orbison, a rock and roll singer from Wink.
____ t. Roy	20. Fawcett, an actress from Port Arthur.
____ u. George	21. Nesmith, a former member of the Monkees.
____ v. Steve	22. Rather, a famous newsman from Houston.
____ w. Boz	23. Hagman, who played J. R. Ewing on "Dallas."
____ x. Clint	24. Mandrell, a singer who had her own TV show.
____ y. Patrick	25. Nelson, a country singer from Abbot.

Farrah

Waylon
Carol
Larry
Tanya

The Great Texas Brand Challenge

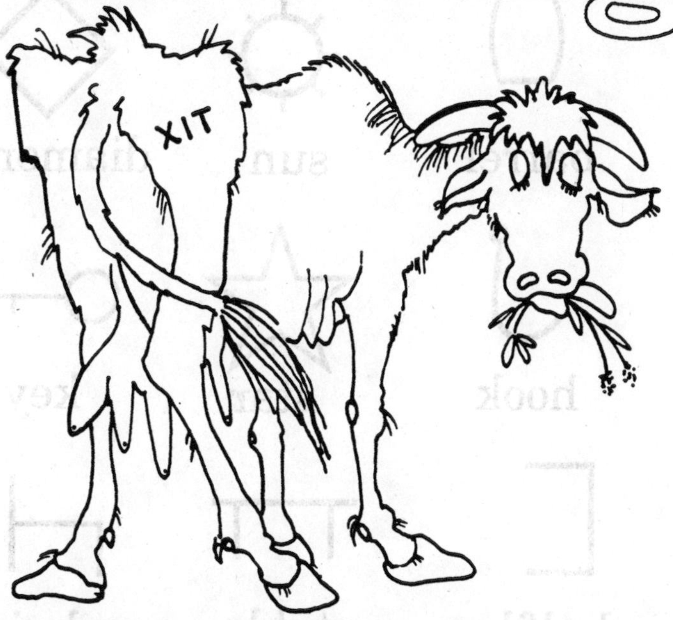
XIT

If you lived on a ranch and owned thousands of cows, how do you suppose you would know for sure which cows were yours? After all, cows do not have license plates like your parents' car, so how would you prove a certain cow was yours if someone else said it was his? The answer is that you would devise a special brand and then burn it into the thick hide of each cow as a form of identification. After branding, there would be no question about who owned the cows.

Cowboys have been branding cattle for about as long as there has been a Texas. There have been so many different brands that you almost have to learn a second language to be able to read them. Just for fun, would you like to know how to read brands? You can easily learn. Then you can amaze your parents if you see a cow with a brand you can read. To learn how to read brands, just follow the easy instructions on the following pages.

The Great Texas Brand Challenge

Cowboys had to be creative when branding their cattle because they did not have time to spell out big words. As a shortcut, the cowboys created many special symbols that could be used in place of words. There were many different kinds of symbols, but the ones below were most common. To learn how to read brands, first study these symbols. Next, study the ways to customize letters and the reading instructions on the next page. When you have finished that, try the Great Texas Brand Reading Challenge on the following page.

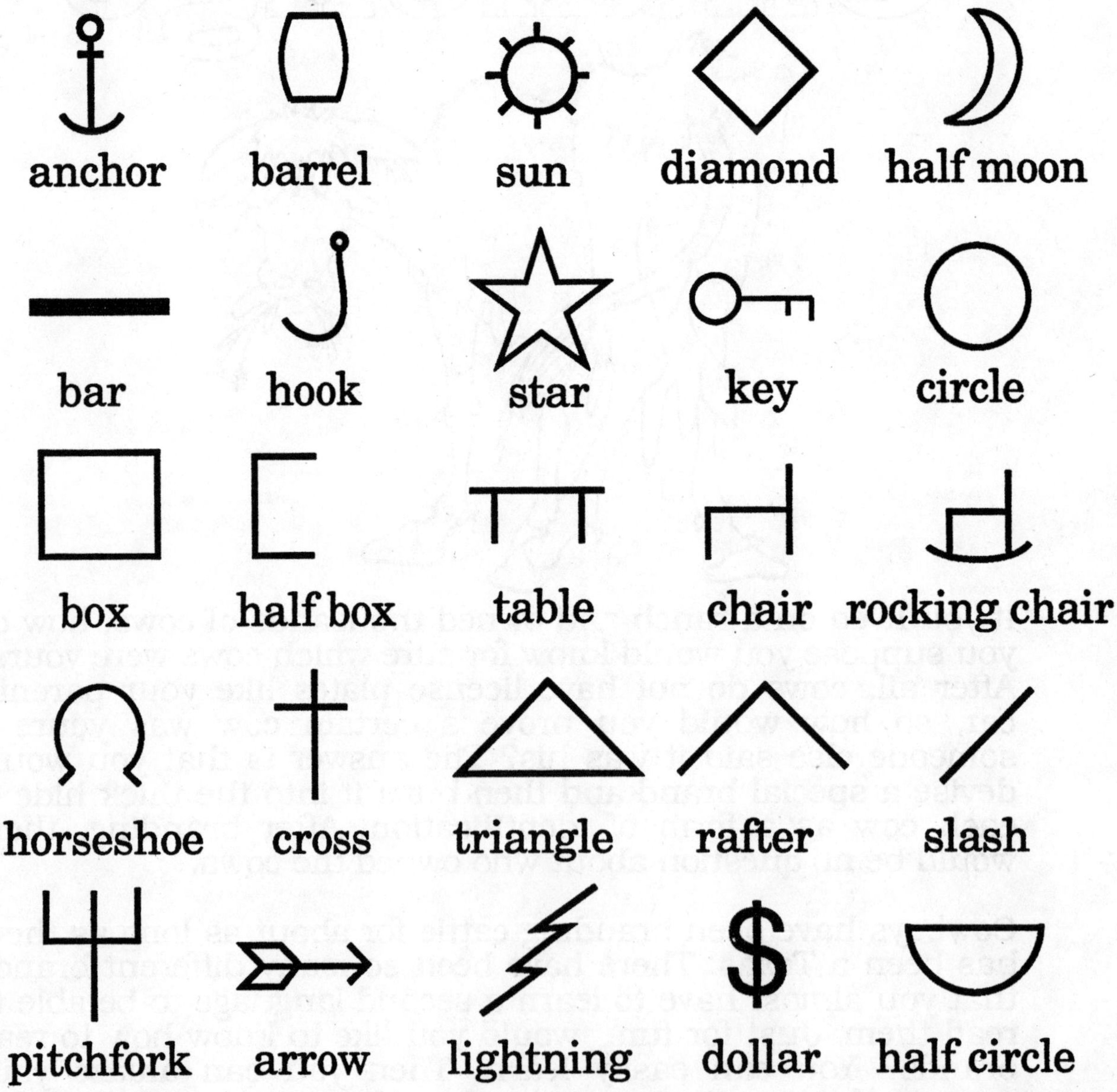
anchor
barrel
sun
diamond
half moon
bar
hook
star
key
circle
box
half box
table
chair
rocking chair
horseshoe
cross
triangle
rafter
slash
pitchfork
arrow
lightning
dollar
half circle

In addition to symbols, there are ways to customize brands for certain special effects as follows:

Adding  makes a letter "flying" so  is flying L.

Adding  makes a letter "walking" so  is walking H.

Adding  makes a letter "forked" so  is forked M.

Adding  makes a letter "hooked" so  is hooked W.

Adding  makes a letter "dragging" so  is dragging L.

Adding  makes a letter "rocking" so  is rocking W.

Adding  makes a letter "swinging" so  is swinging M.

Letters that are leaning are "tumbling" so  is tumbling D.

Letters that are upside down are "crazy" so  is crazy A.

Letters that are laying down are "lazy" so  is lazy B.

Letters drawn backwards are "backward" so  is backward E.

To read a brand, there are some rules to follow:

 Up and down brands are read from top to bottom so this is Bar A.

 Symbols inside symbols are read from the outside in so this is Circle C.

 Side-by-side symbols are read from left to right so this is T Box.

DDD
3D
Some brands look different but are read the same way. Both of these would be Three D.

 Some brands combine several rules in the same design so use the rules in order. This brand would be Box A Diamond.

Ok, now you know how to read brands. It's time to give it a try. The following exercises will test your new skill.

The Great Texas Brand Reading Challenge

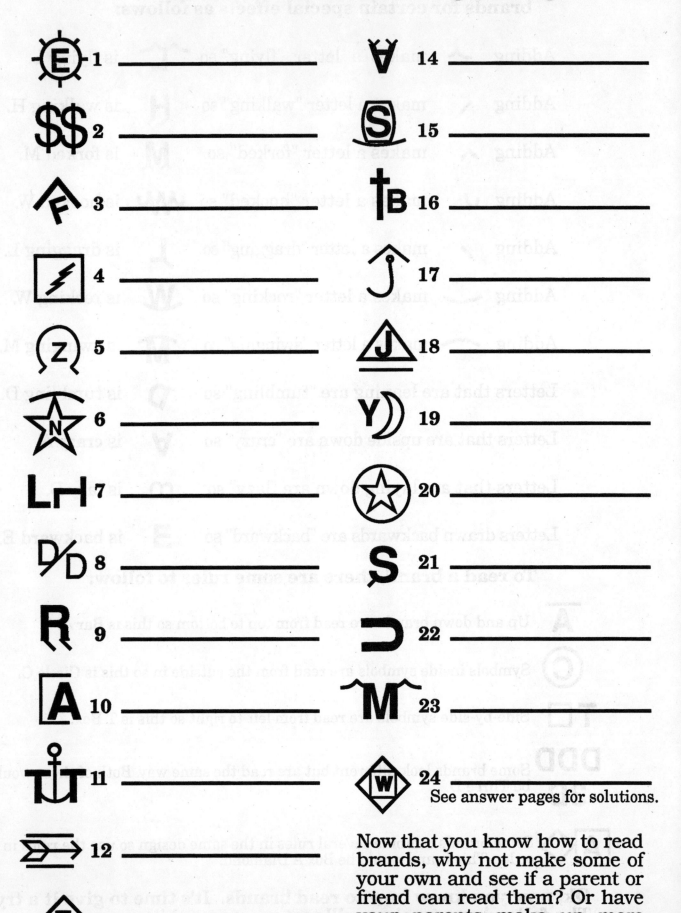

1 ____________________

2 ____________________

3 ____________________

4 ____________________

5 ____________________

6 ____________________

7 ____________________

8 ____________________

9 ____________________

10 ____________________

11 ____________________

12 ____________________

13 ____________________

14 ____________________

15 ____________________

16 ____________________

17 ____________________

18 ____________________

19 ____________________

20 ____________________

21 ____________________

22 ____________________

23 ____________________

24 ____________________

See answer pages for solutions.

Now that you know how to read brands, why not make some of your own and see if a parent or friend can read them? Or have your parents make up more brands for you to read.

Texas Challenge . . .

Know Your State Symbols

The state of Texas has several official state symbols which you should know. Match each symbol on the left with the correct answer on the right. Good luck!

A. ______ Texas state flower

B. ______ Texas state mascot

C. ______ Texas state bird

D. ______ Texas state motto

E. ______ Texas state tree

F. ______ Texas state song

G. ______ Texas state gem

H. ______ Texas state dish

I. ______ Texas state stone

J. ______ Texas state grass

1. *Texas, Our Texas*
2. Don't Mess With Texas
3. Johnson Grass
4. Longhorn steer
5. Bluebonnet
6. Eagle
7. Barbecue
8. Mockingbird
9. Treaty oak tree
10. *The Eyes of Texas*
11. Tyler rose
12. Sideoats gamma grass
13. Pecan tree
14. Palmwood stone
15. Topaz gem
16. Friendship
17. Opal gem
18. Sandstone
19. Armadillo
20. Chili

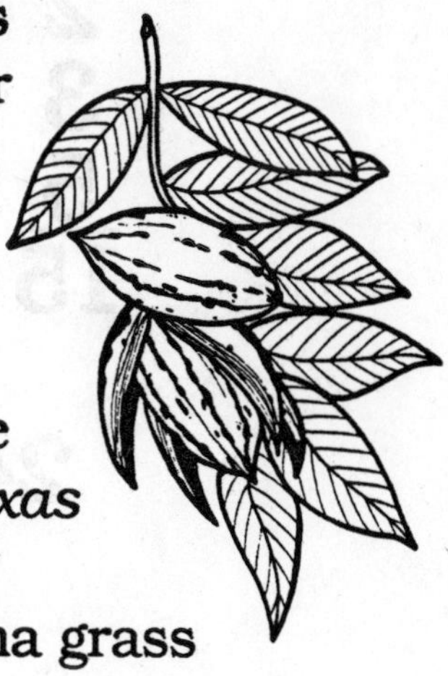

nice plus sum state 2 X 4 = 8 run

The Great Texas Word and Math Challenge

4 + 1 + 2 + 3 + 5 = 15

21 X 3 = 63

24 - 11 = 13 dock 1 + 3 + 2 + 5 = 11

shoot each 2 + 2 = 4 hunt wax

To take this challenge, here is all you do. On the pages that follow, there are several names of Texas towns. Your challenge is to form as many words as possible from the letters in each town name. Try to find as many words as you can to test your vocabulary and spelling!

To test your math skill, you have to score your answers. Each three-letter word you find is worth 3 points, four-letter words are worth 4 points, five-letter words are worth 5 points, and so on. Two-letter words and proper names do not count. To find your score, write the value of each word you make in the small square next to the word and then add up all your scores. If you prefer, count the three-letter words and multiply by 3. Then multiply the number of four-letter words by 4, and so on. Add up your answers for your total score.

Hint: You can challenge a friend or your parents to see who can score the most. If anyone else wants to play, have them list their answers on a separate page and then score the same way. The person with the highest score wins!

Cut 'n Shoot

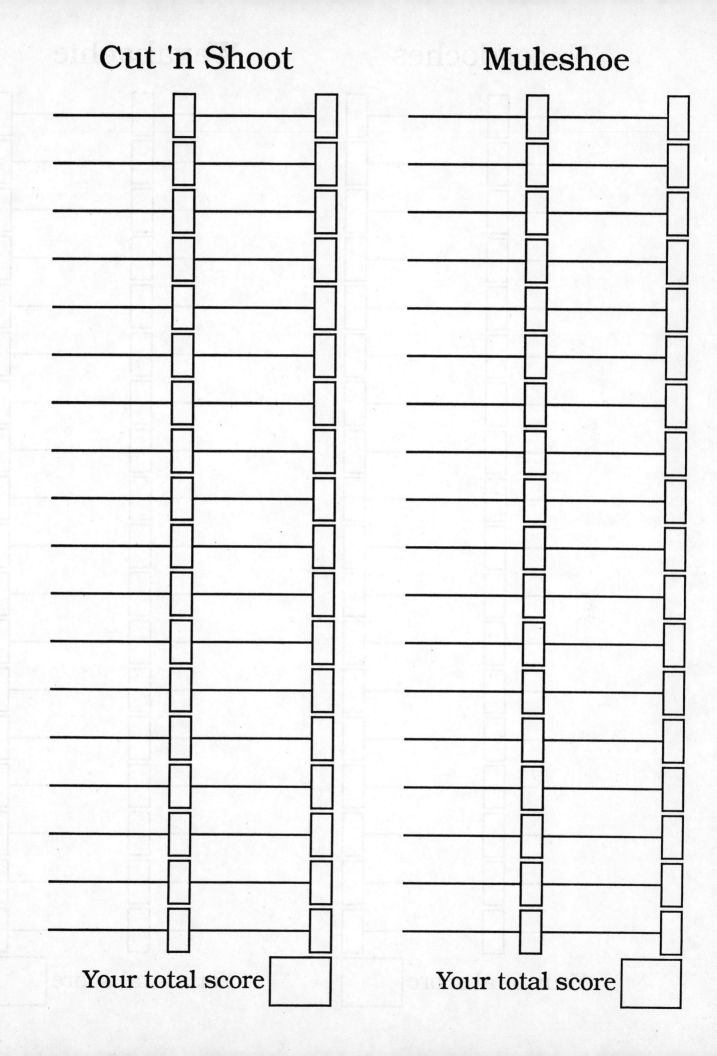

Your total score

Muleshoe

Your total score

Nacogdoches

Your total score

Waxahachie

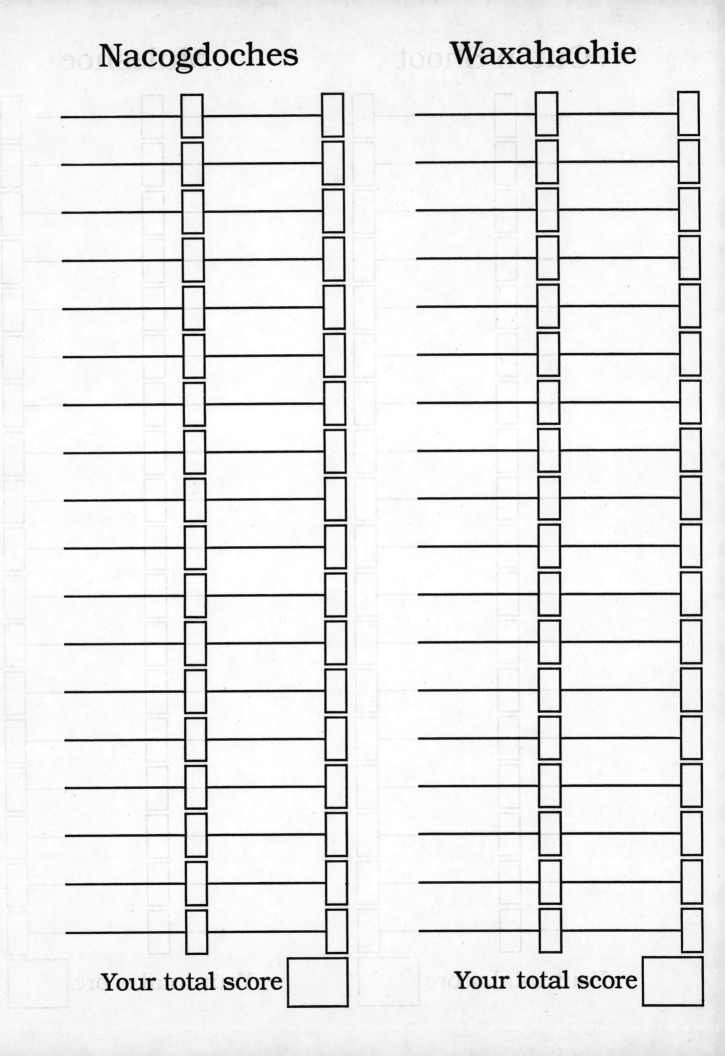

Your total score

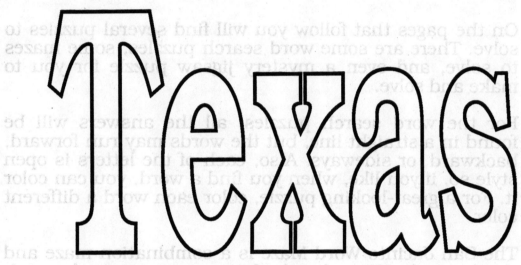

Texas Puzzles

Texas Puzzles

On the pages that follow you will find several puzzles to solve. There are some word search puzzles, some mazes to solve, and even a mystery jigsaw puzzle for you to make and solve.

For the word search puzzles, all the answers will be found in a straight line, but the words may run forward, backward, or sideways. Also, each of the letters is open style so, if you like, when you find a word, you can color it. For a great-looking puzzle, color each word a different color.

The San Jacinto Word Maze is a combination maze and word search. You color the letters as in a word search but you must find the right path for those letters. For the other mazes, all you have to do is begin at "start here" and try to find the one path that will solve the puzzle. Some are easy and some are not so easy.

For the mystery jigsaw puzzle, first remove the entire page and then cut out each individual piece. When that is done, try to put the pieces together to form a picture of something you know very well.

In case you get stuck on any puzzle, the answers are all in the back of the book. Good luck.

San Jacinto Word Maze

On April 21, 1836, General Sam Houston led the Texas army into battle against the Mexican army under General Antonio Lopez de Santa Anna. The Texans charged across a wide plain at a place known as San Jacinto. In just 18 minutes they won the battle and freedom for Texas. As the Texans raced toward victory, they yelled "Remember the Alamo! Remember Goliad!" in honor of their fellow Texas freedom fighters who had died in the Alamo and at Goliad. To solve this maze, start in the upper left-hand corner and find the path that spells the phrase "Remember the Alamo, Remember Goliad" in order. You can change directions within a word, but you cannot skip any letters.

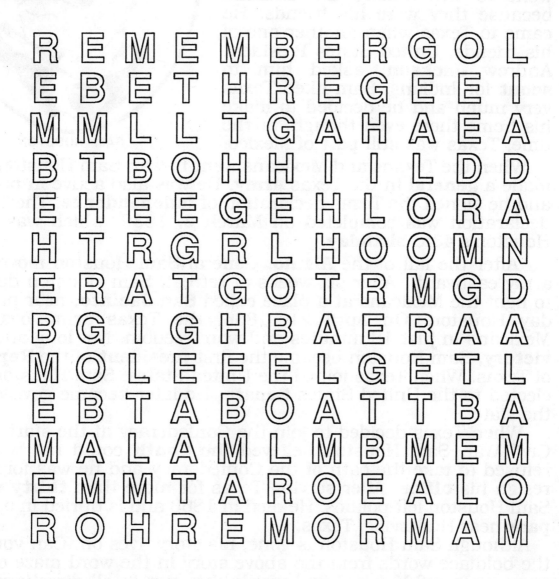

R	E	M	E	M	B	E	R	G	O	L
E	B	E	T	H	R	E	G	E	E	I
M	M	L	L	T	G	A	H	A	E	A
B	T	B	O	H	H	I	I	L	D	D
E	H	E	E	G	E	H	L	O	R	A
H	T	R	G	R	L	H	O	O	M	N
E	R	A	T	G	O	T	R	M	G	D
B	G	I	G	H	B	A	E	R	A	A
M	O	L	E	E	E	L	G	E	T	L
E	B	T	A	B	O	A	T	T	B	A
M	A	L	A	M	L	M	B	M	E	M
E	M	M	T	A	R	O	E	A	L	O
R	O	H	R	E	M	O	R	M	A	M

The Sam Houston Story

SAM HOUSTON

Sam **Houston** was one of the most famous **Texans** of all time. He was born in Tennessee where he was a **lawyer** and a soldier before being elected **governor** of that state. When **Sam** Houston's marriage failed, he went to live among the **Indians** because they were his friends. He came to Texas when another one of his friends, United States President Andrew **Jackson**, asked him to **scout** for Indians. Sam liked Texas very much and he decided to make his home there even though, at the time, Texas was still part of Mexico.

When the Texans and Mexicans went to war, Sam Houston was made a **general** in the Texas **army**. He was also active in politics and he signed the Texas declaration of **independence**. The Texas declaration was completed on March 2, 1836, which was Sam Houston's 43rd **birthday**.

After the fall of the **Alamo**, General Sam Houston moved his army eastward. After six weeks of retreat, Sam Houston decided to fight the Mexicans at a place called **San Jacinto**, near present day Houston. On April 21, 1836, the Texas army beat the Mexicans in just 18 minutes and won freedom. Not long after the **victory**, Sam Houston became the first **president** of the **Republic** of Texas. When Texas joined the United States, Sam Houston was elected to the United States **Senate**. He later became governor of the state.

When Texas decided to join the Confederacy at the start of the Civil War, Sam Houston believed the **South** could not win. He refused to take the oath of the Confederacy and he was forced to resign his **office**. After serving Texas for more than **thirty** years, Sam Houston left politics. He died in 1863 and is buried in a small **park** near Huntsville, Texas.

Although Sam Houston is gone, his story lives on. Can you find the boldface words from the above story in the word maze on the opposite page? You will find words that run in all directions, but they will always be in a straight line.

The Sam Houston Story

N	A	B	Y	T	R	I	H	T	C	W	T	A	I
O	A	F	A	B	O	B	S	D	A	T	X	C	N
T	F	S	C	G	E	N	N	Z	C	U	S	O	D
S	N	A	X	E	T	V	A	L	A	N	O	T	E
U	T	U	O	C	S	I	I	D	T	B	U	N	P
O	E	D	F	E	C	C	D	A	N	S	T	I	E
H	E	L	S	R	F	T	N	Z	N	R	H	C	N
A	C	B	A	A	B	O	I	F	O	E	W	A	D
H	N	I	M	W	Z	R	S	N	S	T	C	J	A
T	E	R	C	F	Y	Y	R	B	K	A	F	N	N
N	D	E	A	G	D	E	M	R	C	N	Q	A	T
E	N	P	J	D	V	Y	R	M	A	E	R	S	N
D	E	U	X	O	A	K	I	A	J	S	A	M	E
I	P	B	G	E	N	E	R	A	L	L	B	A	C
S	E	L	B	U	Q	L	F	R	A	C	P	P	I
E	D	I	A	P	A	R	K	M	M	A	L	O	F
R	N	C	V	I	C	T	O	Y	R	C	N	A	F
P	I	F	C	Y	B	I	R	T	H	D	A	Y	O

Texas Animals

There are lots of different kinds of animals in Texas. Can you find the animals pictured on these two pages in the puzzle?

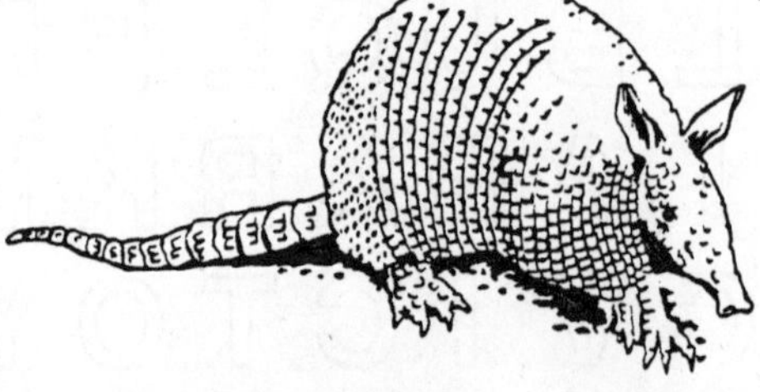

Texas Animals

L	A	B	R	O	A	D	R	U	N	N	E	R
O	S	T	A	F	G	E	B	D	H	K	L	D
N	L	T	B	D	H	Z	S	I	D	K	G	E
G	L	L	B	A	S	S	E	G	R	K	Y	S
H	P	Q	I	X	N	T	G	R	I	Z	E	R
O	L	A	T	D	O	T	S	A	B	L	K	O
R	J	W	O	Y	A	N	H	K	G	O	R	H
N	V	V	O	T	R	M	A	I	N	P	U	Y
S	E	C	H	C	E	F	R	I	I	T	T	L
R	A	T	T	L	E	S	N	A	K	E	O	T
G	D	U	T	E	D	O	P	T	C	J	K	E
D	R	I	B	G	N	I	K	C	O	M	K	E
J	D	T	A	O	G	N	H	C	M	L	H	I

The Alamo Heroes

On Sunday morning, March 6, 1836, after a thirteen day siege, General Santa Anna's Mexican army stormed the Alamo in San Antonio and killed more than 180 Texas defenders. Although Santa Anna won the battle, he lost more than six-hundred troops.

No one knows exactly how many Texans lost their lives that sad morning. The following men were among the Texans who fell. Can you find their last names in the puzzle on the opposite page? Remember, you might find the names going up, down, sideways, or backwards, but you will always find them in a straight line. Good luck!

1. William B. **Travis**
2. James **Bowie**
3. Davy **Crockett**
4. James **Bonham**
5. Green B. **Jameson**
6. Capt. A. **Dickinson**
7. Albert **Martin**
8. Daniel **Cloud**
9. William **Blazeby**
10. Issac **Millsaps**
11. Asa **Walker**
12. Tapley **Holland**
13. John **Baugh**
14. Micajah **Autry**
15. Amos **Pollard**
16. Joseph **Kerr**
17. John **Gavin**
18. James **Ewing**
19. James **Brown**
20. Lewis **Duel**
21. William **Parks**
22. William **Carey**
23. Juan **Badillo**
24. William **King**

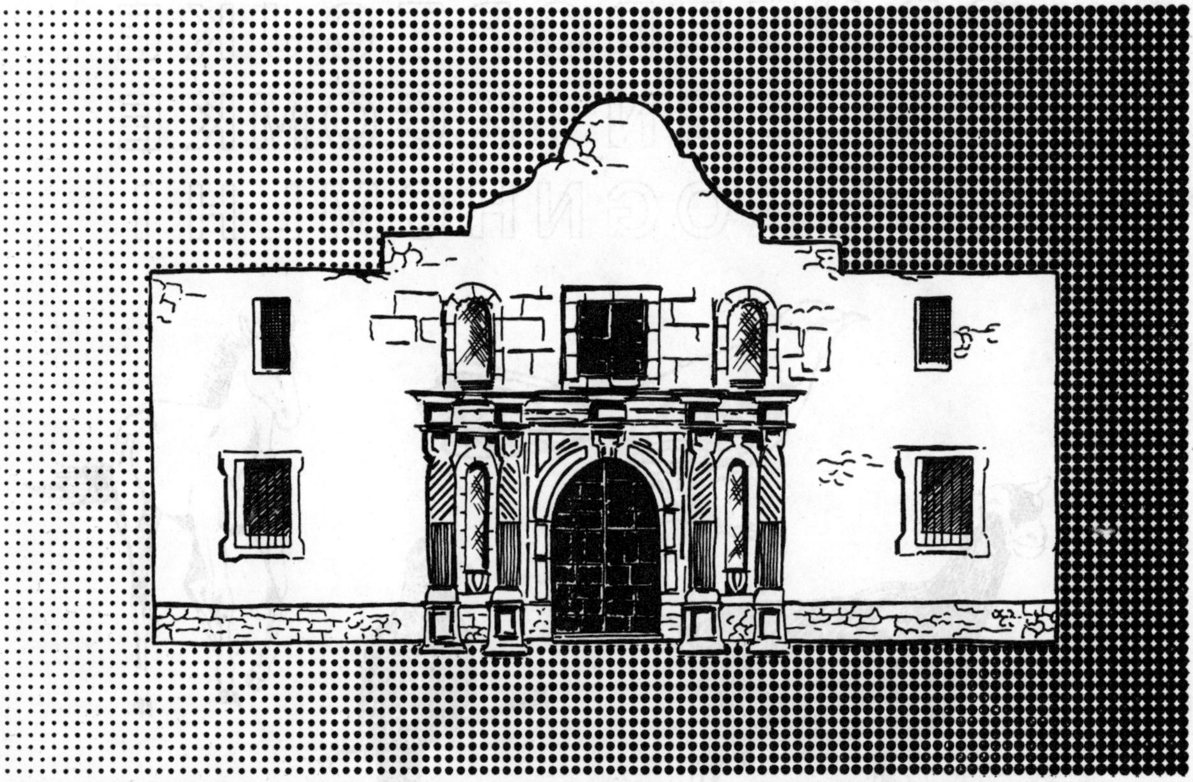

The Alamo Heroes

N	O	S	E	M	A	J	H	C	J	G	Y	B	B
O	N	S	T	A	B	A	O	R	S	A	E	P	B
E	J	T	Y	D	U	E	L	O	P	V	R	R	A
I	B	R	R	M	G	M	L	C	A	I	A	C	N
W	U	A	T	A	H	S	A	K	S	N	C	O	R
O	O	V	U	R	V	O	N	E	L	S	S	T	L
B	L	S	A	T	D	I	D	T	L	N	E	R	G
B	C	I	A	I	K	N	S	C	I	W	F	N	I
A	C	V	E	N	K	T	D	K	M	A	I	M	N
U	R	K	E	R	R	R	C	R	E	K	L	A	W
G	O	O	Y	F	I	I	E	D	K	L	A	D	O
H	C	E	B	K	D	F	K	U	X	E	T	E	R
G	K	L	E	B	R	R	B	O	N	H	A	M	B
A	E	P	Z	C	A	R	R	L	N	O	P	E	P
V	T	R	A	P	L	K	M	C	R	R	T	L	U
E	T	A	L	C	L	T	E	W	I	N	G	T	B
N	S	K	B	M	O	B	A	D	I	L	L	O	X
K	R	A	P	P	P	J	U	W	S	K	R	A	P

The Lost San Saba Mine Maze

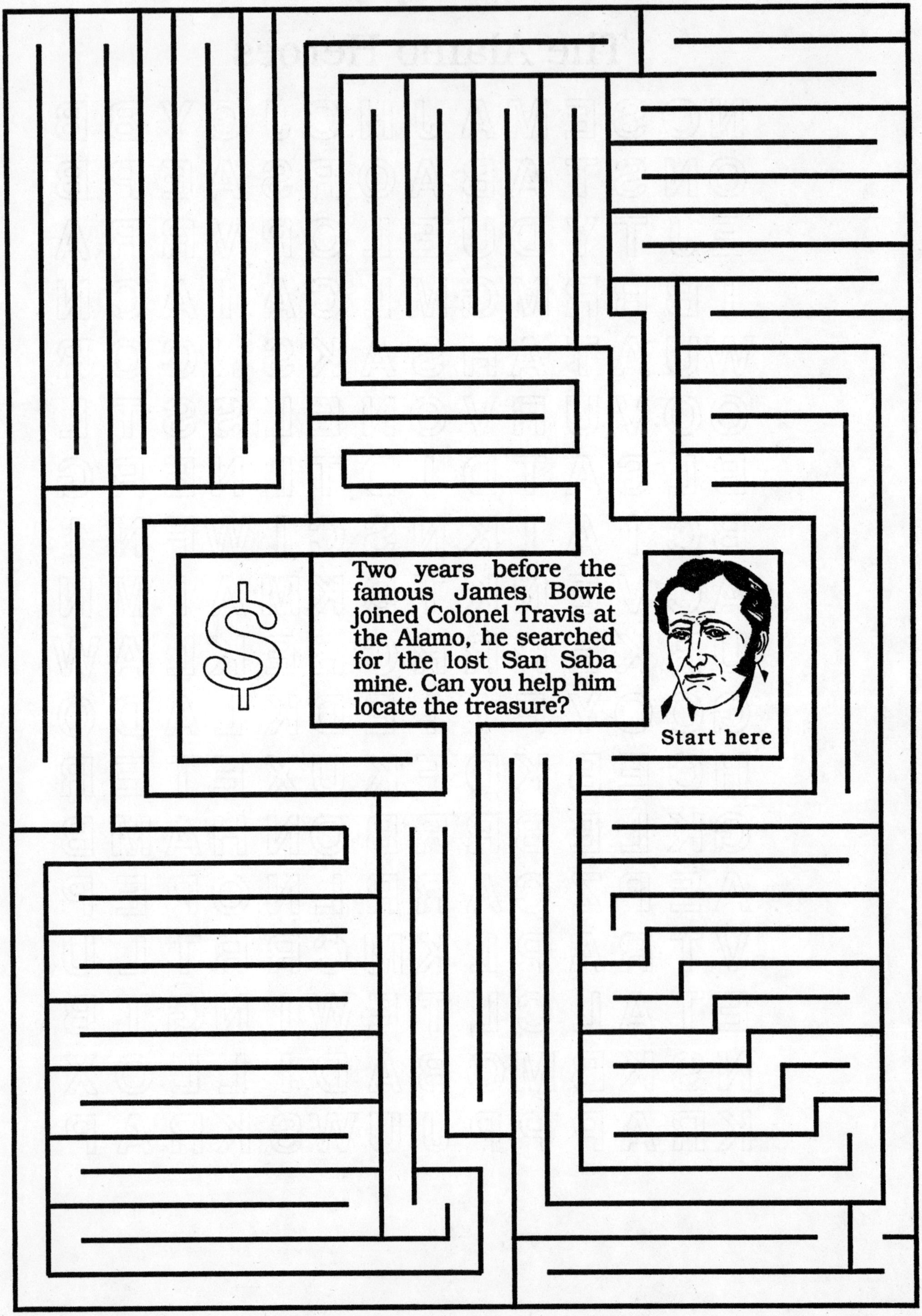
Two years before the famous James Bowie joined Colonel Travis at the Alamo, he searched for the lost San Saba mine. Can you help him locate the treasure?
Start here

The Davy Crockett Maze

In 1836, Davy Crockett resigned from the United States Senate and came to Texas to explore new land. He arrived in Nacogdoches in January and joined the Texas army as a private. He soon left to join Colonel Travis at the Alamo. Can you help Davy find his way?

Start here

The Texas Dinosaur Maze

Thousands of years ago, dinosaurs roamed over Texas. Some of the big footprints those animals left behind can still be seen around Glen Rose, Texas. Do you think you can help this dinosaur find Glen Rose so he can make some tracks?

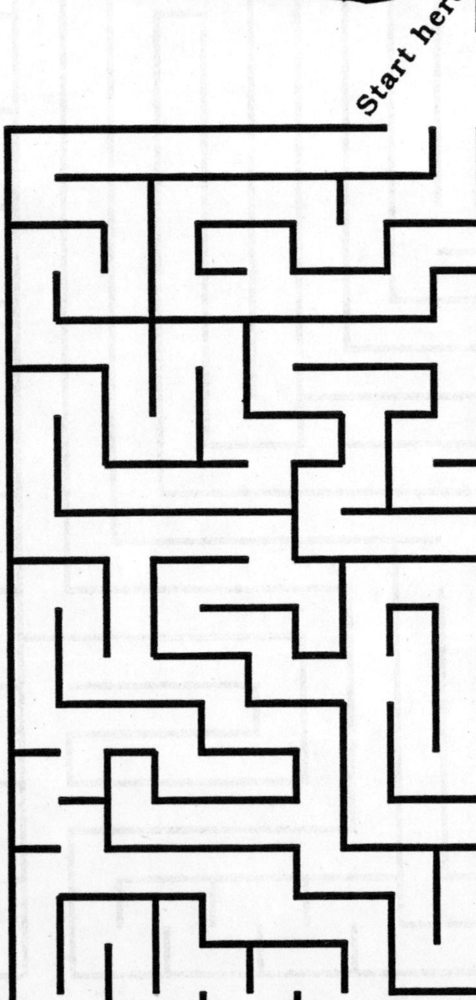
Start here

Glen Rose,
Texas

The Lost Prairie Dog Maze

Prairie Dog Town
Lubbock, Texas

About one hundred years ago, there were millions of prairie dogs in West Texas. Today, they are a little hard to find unless you are in Lubbock, Texas, where there is an entire prairie dog town. This little prairie dog has gotten lost. Can you help him find his way back to prairie dog town?

Start here

Mystery Puzzle

To solve this puzzle, remove this page and paste it on posterboard, then cut out the pieces. Fit them together to discover the mystery shape. The solution is in the back of the book.

Texas

Projects

Texas Projects

On the pages that follow you will find several projects to make including some signs for your room and a special "Growing Tall in Texas" wall chart. Almost every project has some parts for you to color, so have fun.

Please be sure to follow some special rules:

When you get out materials to make a project, be sure to put them away when you are finished.

Please do not use any of your parents' materials for these projects without asking permission first. You wouldn't want anyone using your materials without asking, would you?

Many of the projects in this section are designed to be hung on the wall. Please, do not hang anything on a wall unless you ask permission first. Never, ever use nails, tape, tacks, or push pins unless your parents say it is OK.

Make-UR-Own

Growing TALL In Texas Chart

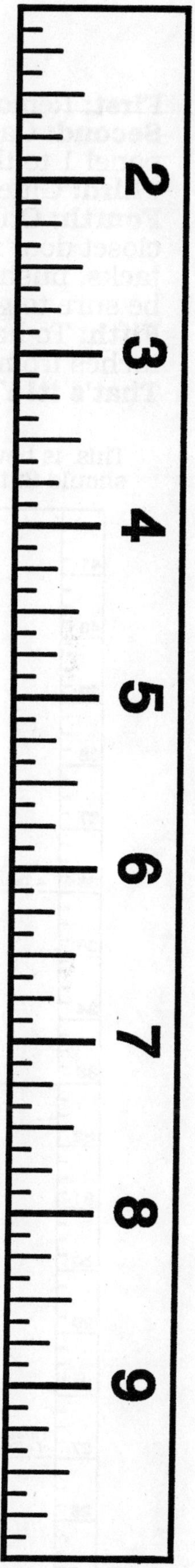
2
3
4
5
6
7
8
9

Growing Tall in Texas Chart

Instructions and Suggestions

First: Remove the following pages of "Growing Tall in Texas" chart panels.
Second: Carefully cut out panel number 1 and panel number 2. Glue the top of panel 1 to the bottom of panel 2 as shown.
Third: Glue the remaining panels in place to complete the chart.
Fourth: Once your chart is complete, find a place to hang it. The inside of a closet door makes a wonderful spot. Note, you can hang your chart with tape, tacks, push pins, or poster putty but before making any holes in a wall or door, be sure to get your parents permission.
Fifth: To hang your chart, put the line marked "Bottom of Chart" exactly 24 inches from the floor.
That's it! Your chart is now ready to use!

This is how your panels should fit together.

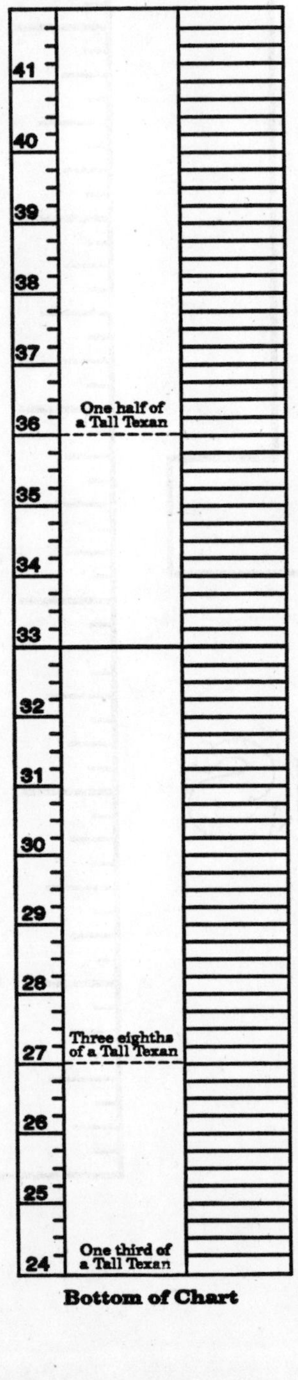
41
40
39
38
37
One half of a Tall Texan
36
35
34
33
32
31
30
29
28
Three eighths of a Tall Texan
27
26
25
One third of a Tall Texan
24
Bottom of Chart

How to use your new chart

To record your height you will need a ruler, a pencil, and help from a parent. Stand up straight in front of the chart and ask one of your parents to hold the ruler level on top of your head and mark your height in the ruler section of the chart. Then, you use a crayon or colored pencil and color in the ruler section below your present height. Write the date you were measured in the note section of the chart.

You will want to be measured two or three times a year to see how much you are growing. Select certain times to be measured, such as your birthday, Christmas, the end of school, etc. Each time you are measured, use a different color in the ruler section to show how much you have grown since the last time you were measured. Always write the date you are measured so you will have a good record of your growth.

Special Hints

You might want to be measured on the last day of each school year and then glue one of your school pictures in the center section of the chart. That way you will have a record of how you changed as you grew taller!

Each time you are measured, write about something special in your life at the time in the note section of the chart. You could write the name of your current boy or girl friend, your favorite sports hero, or whatever you like.

For fun, you can measure Mom and Dad on your chart so you can see how much more you have to grow to be as tall as your parents.

Growing Tall in Texas, strip 1

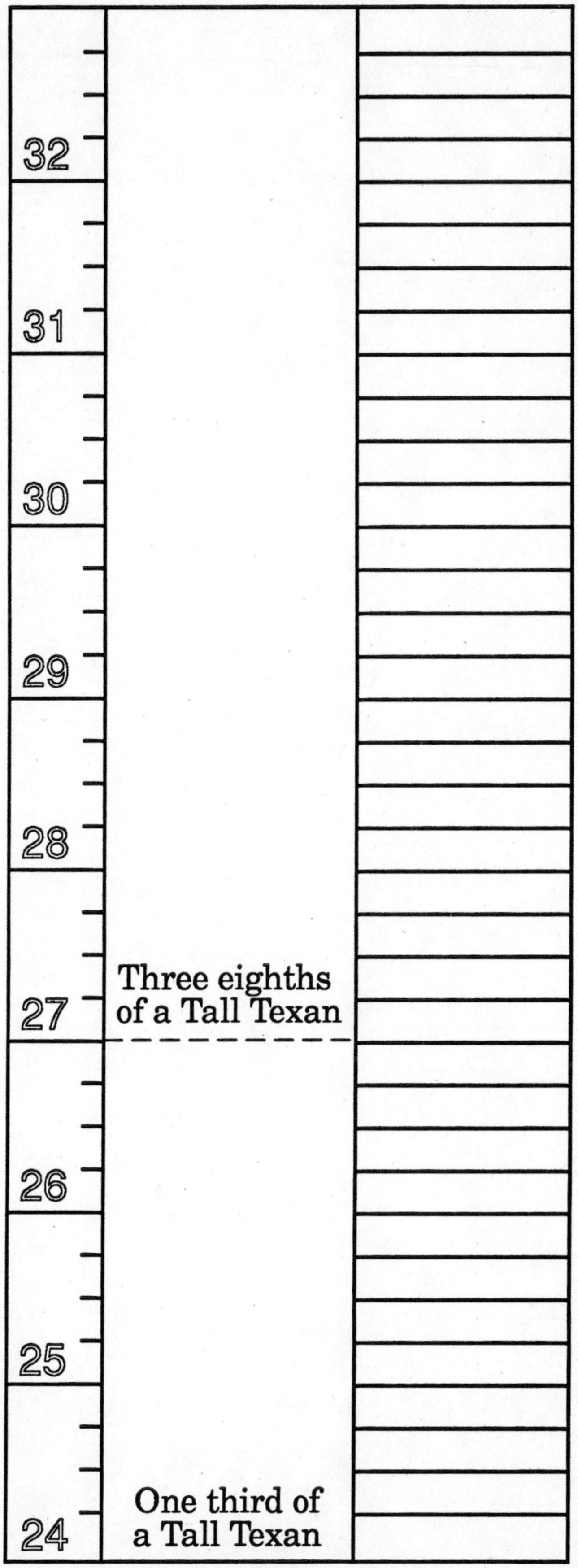
32
31
30
29
28
Three eighths
of a Tall Texan
27
26
25
One third of
a Tall Texan
24

Bottom of Chart

Growing Tall in Texas, strip 2

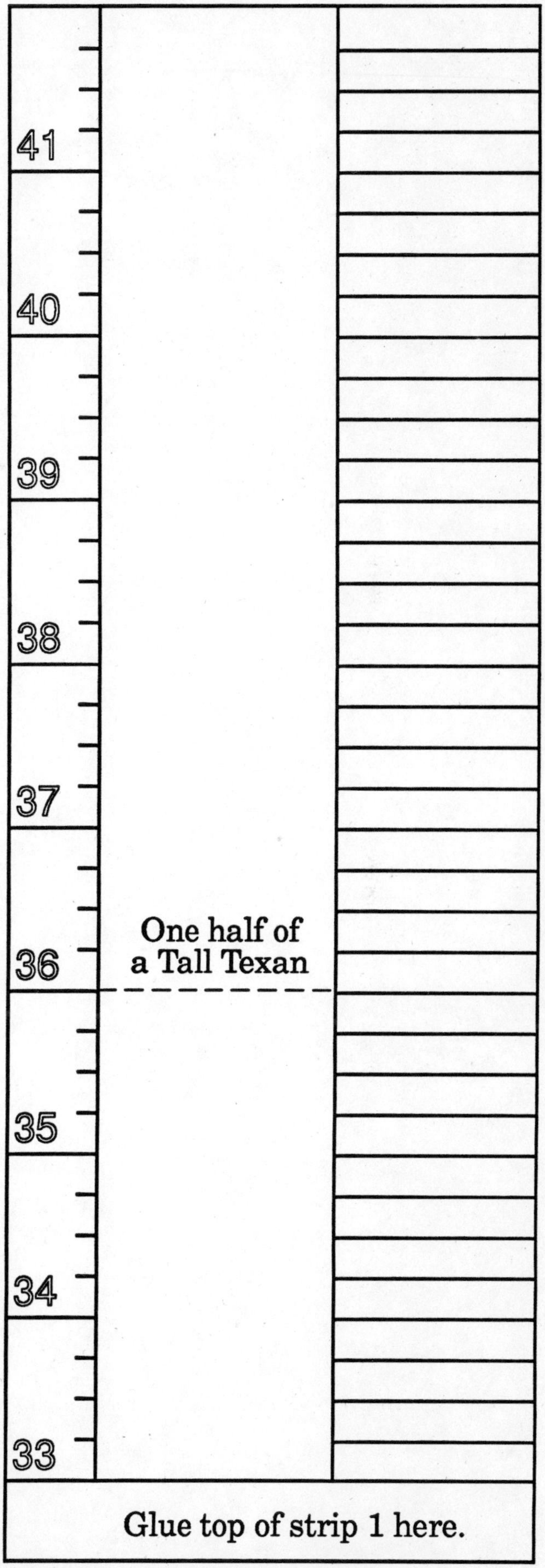
41
40
39
38
37
One half of
a Tall Texan
36
35
34
33
Glue top of strip 1 here.

Growing Tall in Texas, strip 3

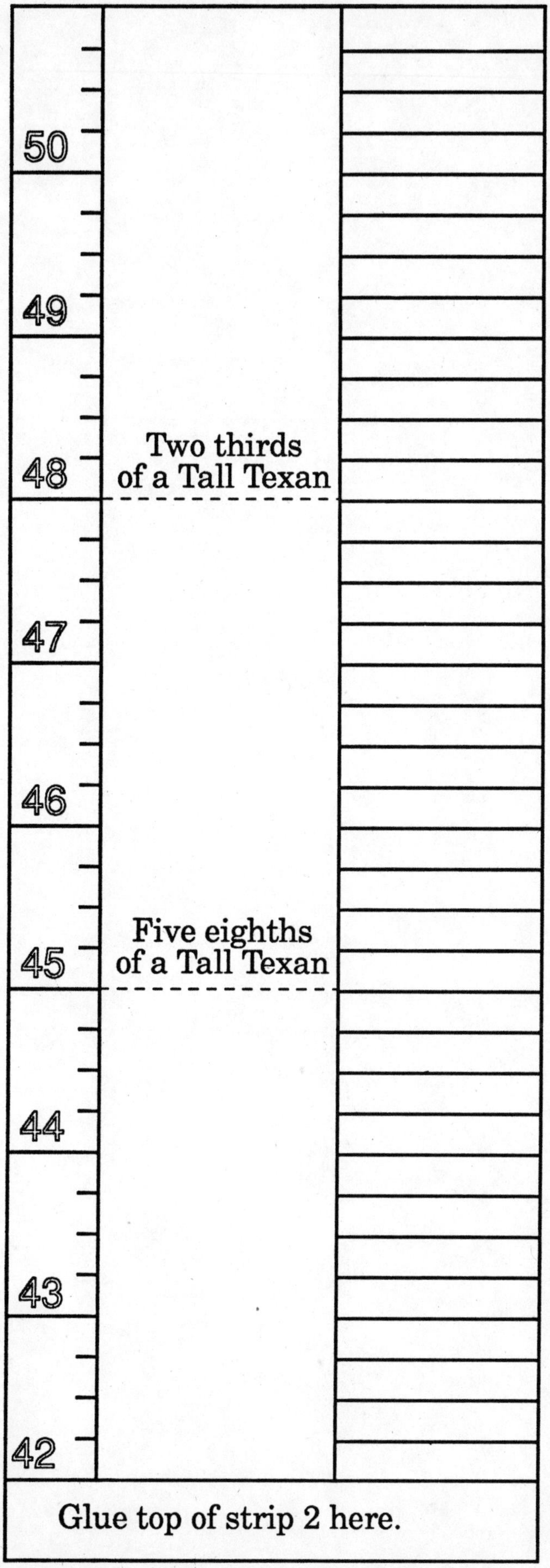
50
49
Two thirds
of a Tall Texan
48
47
46
Five eighths
of a Tall Texan
45
44
43
42
Glue top of strip 2 here.

Growing Tall in Texas, strip 4

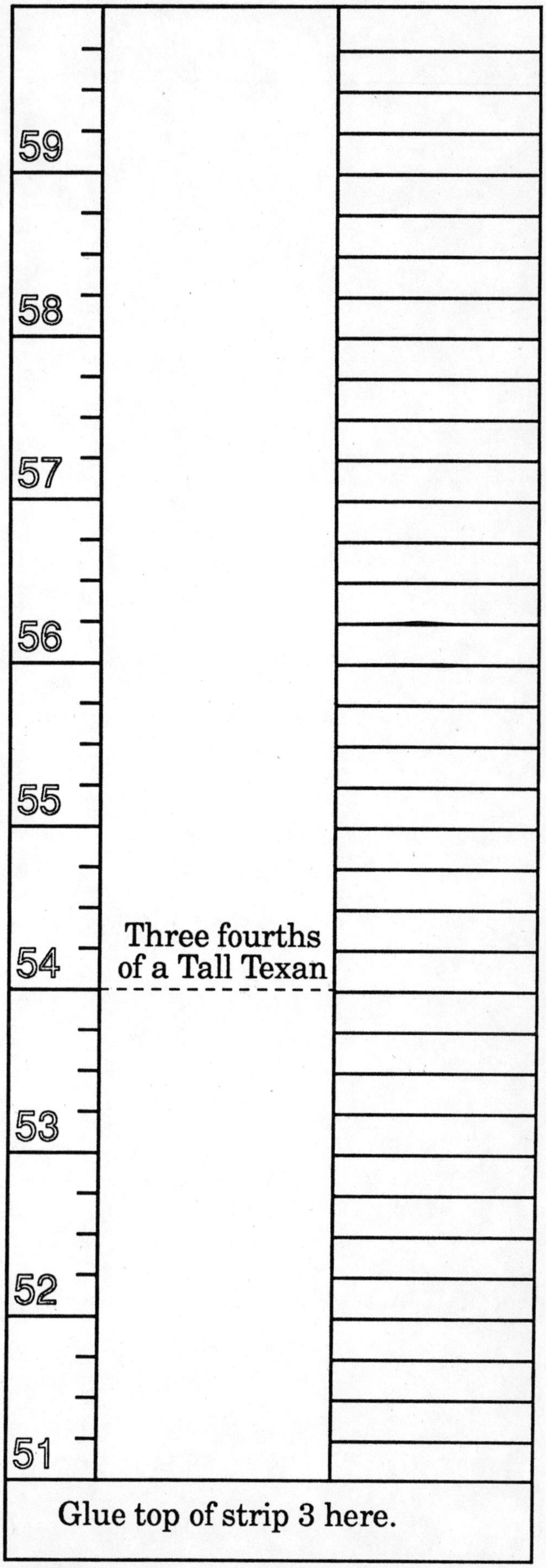
59
58
57
56
55
Three fourths
of a Tall Texan
54
53
52
51
Glue top of strip 3 here.

Growing Tall in Texas, strip 5

68

67 The height of Audie Murphy, the bravest Texan of all time.

66

65

64

63 Seven eighths of a Tall Texan

62

61

60

Glue top of strip 4 here.

Growing Tall in Texas, strip 6

Growing Tall In Texas

This Chart belongs to:

76

75

74

73

72 A Tall Texan

71

70

69

Glue top of strip 5 here.

Make UR Own

Room Signs

Here is a collection of signs you can make for your room. All you do is carefully cut out each sign and then color them as you like. To add strength to your signs you can mount them on poster board before hanging. Also, remember the rule about never hanging anything without first asking permission.

In addition to signs for your room door, there are also some hangers which will fit over the knob on a door. You make these the same way as the signs but you really should mount them on poster board before you cut them out so they will be strong and last a long time.

Don't mess with Texas

[or this room]

CAUTION
OFFICIAL STATE OF TEXAS
DIRT TEST AREA
DO NOT
CLEAN

This room belongs to

Please Do Not
Mess With It!!

DISASTER AREA

Enter at your own risk!

STOP

***please* .... knock before entering.**

BOYS
ONLY

GIRLS
ONLY

Make-UR-Own: Door Hangers

INSTRUCTIONS: First, color the signs you want to make. Next, remove the page and paste it on poster board. Last, cut out around the sign and that's it. When finished, hang on your door knob.

CAUTION
HOMEWORK
IN PROGRESS
DO NOT
ENTER

QUIET
PLEASE
I AM
ON THE
PHONE

Make-UR-Own: Door Hangers

INSTRUCTIONS: First, color the signs you want to make. Next, remove the page and paste it on poster board. Last, cut out around the sign and that's it. When finished, hang on your door knob.

Welcome
Home
DAD
We Missed
You Very
Much.

Welcome
Home
MOM
We Missed
You Very
Much.

Make-UR-Own: Door Hangers

INSTRUCTIONS: First, color the signs you want to make. Next, remove the page and paste it on poster board. Last, cut out around the sign and that's it. When finished, hang on your door knob.

please
Do
Not
Disturb
Use this blank to create your own door hanger.

Texas

Answers

Page 9. There are 254 counties in Texas

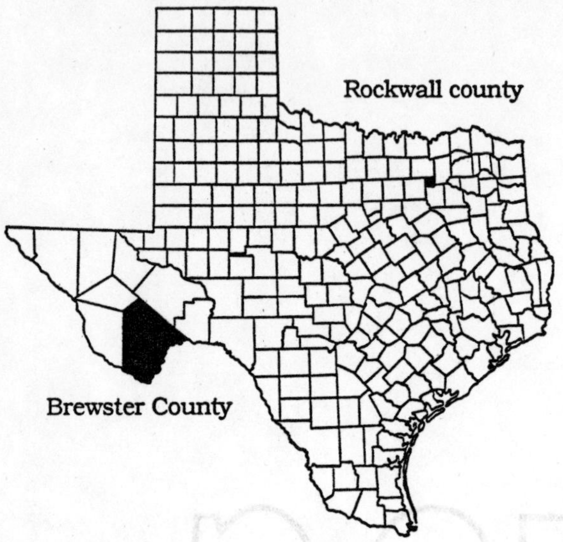
Rockwall county
Brewster County

Page 47

Grand Totals for all Go Rounds.

Bull Riding	215	200	195	225	185
Bronc Riding +	175	215	185	210	225
Bareback +	205	165	235	200	175
Steer Wrestle -	57	63	55	95	85
Barrel Race -	80	75	70	90	65
Grand Total =	458	442	490	450	435

Page 99 Texas Alphabet Soup

1. Stephen F. Austin
2. The X I T ranch
3. Today, the King Ranch
4. Davy Crockett
5. Quana Parker
6. Tejas
7. Yellow.
8. Old Zapata
9. "Lone Star State."
10. Washington, Texas.
11. Under six flags.
12. The Largemouth bass
13. NASA
14. Tom Landry
15. rodeo.
16. Missions.
17. The Apache Indians
18. Lyndon B. Johnson
19. The Davis Mountains
20. The Armadillo
21. Pancho Villa
22. The Texas Rangers
23. The Horned frog
24. A lot of Pine trees
25. "Everybody is somebody."
26. Rio Grande valley.

Page 101 Texas Sports Challenge

1. The Texas **LONGHORNS**
2. The SMU MUSTANGS
3. The MAVERICKS
4. The Houston OILERS
5. The Texas Tech RED RAIDERS
6. The SIDEKICKS
7. The SPURS
8. Texas A&M AGGIES
9. The Rice OWLS
10. The Houston ROCKETS
11. TOM Landry
12. BUM Phillips
13. The Texas RANGERS
14. The RAZORBACKS
15. The TCU HORNED FROGS
16. The Baylor BEARS
17. The Houston COUGARS
18. Dallas COWBOYS
19. The Houston ASTROS

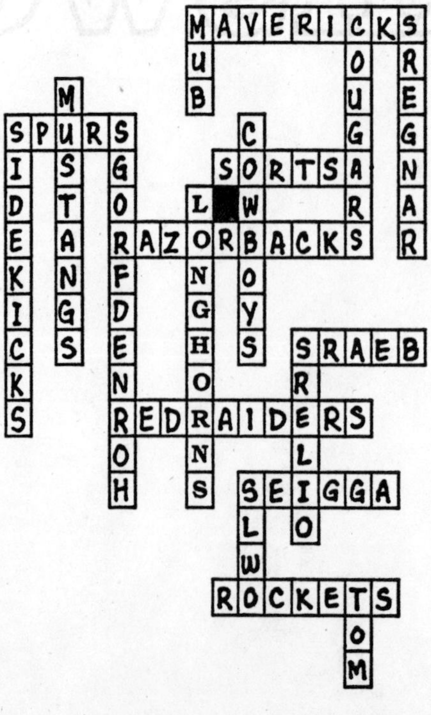

Page 102 Texas Stars

12 a. Carol
8 b. Stevie Ray
5 c. Sandy
10 d. Buddy
13 e. Waylon
17 f. Tanya
20 g. Farrah
22 h. Dan
25 i. Willie
4 j. Freddie
18 k. Kenny
21 l. Michael
1 m. Lee
23 n. Larry
16 o. Mac
6 p. Randy
14 q. Leeza
3 r. Tommy Lee
24 s. Barbara
19 t. Roy
9 u. George
15 v. Steve
11 w. Boz
2 x. Clint
7 y. Patrick

Page 106
The Great Texas Brand Reading Challenge

1. Sun E
2. Double Dollar
3. Rafter Tumbling F
4. Box Lightning
5. Horseshoe Z
6. Swinging Star N
7. L Chair
8. D Slash D
9. Walking R
10. Half Box A
11. T Anchor T
12. Bar Arrow Bar
13. Diamond T
14. Forked Crazy A
15. Rocking Barrel S
16. Cross B
17. Rafter Hook
18. Triangle J Bar
19. Y Half Moon
20. Circle Star
21. Dragging S
22. Lazy U
23. Flying M
24. Diamond Box W

Page 107
State Symbols

A. 5 Texas state flower
B. 19 Texas state mascot
C. 8 Texas state bird
D. 16 Texas state motto
E. 13 Texas state tree
F. 1 Texas state song
G. 17 Texas state gem
H. 20 Texas state dish
I. 14 Texas state stone
J. 12 Texas state grass

Page 113
San Jacinto Word Maze

```
R E M E M B E R G O L
E B E T H R E G E E I
M M L L T G A H A E A
B T B O H H I I L D D
E H E E G E H L O R A
H T R G R L H O O M N
E R A T G O T R M G D
B G I G H B A E R A A
M O L E E E L G E T L
E B T A B O A T T B A
M A L A M L M B M E M
E M M T A R O E A L O
R O H R E M O R M A M
```

Page 115
The Sam Houston Story

```
N A B Y T R I H T C W T A I
O A F A B O B S D A T X C N
T F S C G E N N Z C U S O D
S N A X E T V A L A N O T E
U T U O C S I I D T B U N P
O E D F E C C D A N S T I E
H E L S R F T N Z N R H C N
A C B A A B O I F O E W A D
H N I M W Z R S N S T C J A
T E R C F Y Y R B K A F N N
N D E A G D E M R C N Q A T
E N P J D V Y R M A E R S N
D E U X O A K I A J S A M E
I P B G E N E R A L L B A C
S E L B U Q L F R A C P P I
E D I A P A R K M M A L O F
R N C V I C T O Y R C N A F
P I F C Y B I R T H D A Y O
```

Page 117
Texas Animals

```
L A B R O A D R U N N E R
O S T A F G E B D H K L D
N L T B D H Z S I D K G E
G L L B A S S E G R K Y S
H P Q I X N T G R I Z E R
O L A T D O T S A B L K O
R J W O Y A N H K G O R H
N V V O T R M A I N P U Y
S E C H C E F R I I T T L
R A T T L E S N A K E O T
G D U T E D O P T C J K E
D R I B G N I K C O M K E
J D T A O G N H C M L H I
```

Page 119
The Alamo Heroes

NOSEMAJHCJGYBB
ONSTABAORSAEPB
EJTYDUELOPVRRA
IBRRMGMLCAIACN
WUATAHSAKSNCOR
OOVURVONELSSTL
BLSATDIDTLNERG
BCIAIKNSCIWFNI
ACVENKTDKMAIMN
URKERRRCREKLAW
GOOYFIIEDKLADO
HCEBKDFKUXETER
GKLEBRRBONHAMB
AEPZCARRLNOPEP
VTRAPLKMCRRTLU
ETALCLTEWINGTB
NSKBMOBADILLOX
KRAPPPJUWSKRAP

Page 120
The Lost San Saba Mine Maze

Two years before the famous James Bowie joined Colonel Travis at the Alamo, he searched for the lost San Saba mine. Can you help him locate the treasure?
Start here

Page 121
The Davy Crockett Maze

In 1836, Davy Crockett resigned from the United States Senate and came to Texas to explore new land. He arrived in Nacogdoches in January and joined the Texas army as a private. He soon left to join Colonel Travis at the Alamo. Can you help Davy find his way?
Start here

Page 122
The Texas Dinosaur Maze

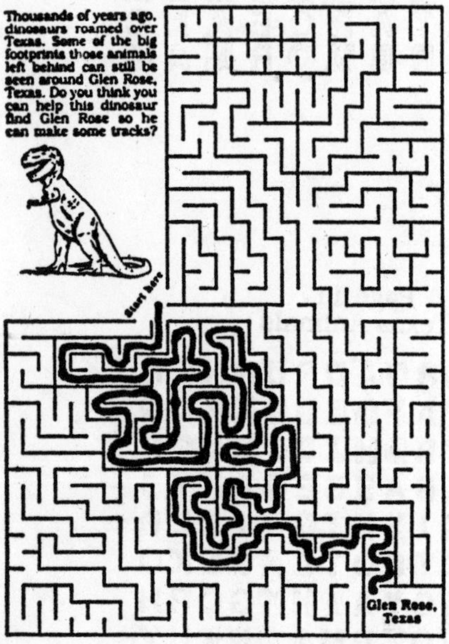
Thousands of years ago, dinosaurs roamed over Texas. Some of the big footprints those animals left behind can still be seen around Glen Rose, Texas. Do you think you can help this dinosaur find Glen Rose so he can make some tracks?
Start here
Glen Rose, Texas

Page 123
The Lost Prairie Dog Maze

Prairie Dog Town
Lubbock, Texas
About one hundred years ago, there were millions of prairie dogs in West Texas. Today, they are a little hard to find unless you are in Lubbock, Texas, where there is an entire prairie dog town. This little prairie dog has gotten lost. Can you help him find his way back to prairie dog town?
Start here

Page 125
Mystery Puzzle

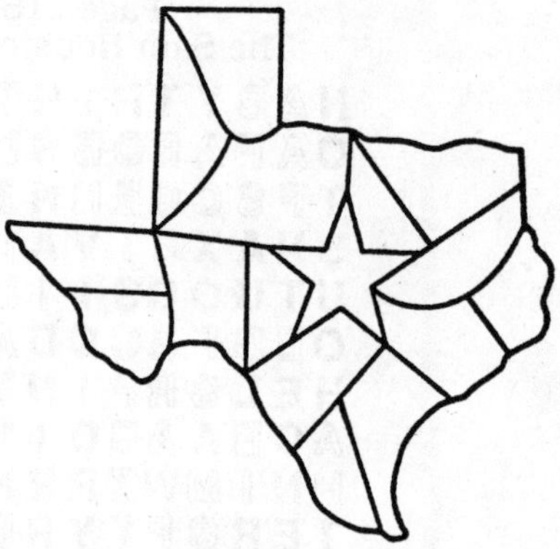